MOUNTAINTOP EXPERIENCE IN THE MIDST OF THE VALLEY

A story of God's amazing peace throughout marital infidelity, a pending divorce and other trials that we encounter

By: Wendy Bordelon

Introduction

Have you ever felt alone and that no one cares? Do you feel that no one could possibly understand what you are going through? Do you find yourself living in the past or regretting decisions that you have made? Do you wish you could change your current circumstances? Do you wish that you could change someone in your life to fit what you think they should be? Do you make up excuses for the choices that you have made? Do you blame others for your circumstances? Do you want to feel loved? Do you want to feel free from all of the burdens and pressures of life?

Last year, I went as a chaperone with our youth group on a canoe trip. I had not been on a canoe trip in over 20 years so my memory was a little fuzzy about the need to be fit. We left at 4:30am to reach our destination and it was miserably hot. (It was mid-summer in Louisiana.) Some of the girls kept turning over their canoe and another female chaperone and I would turn their canoe back over for them. (Canoes can get heavy when they are full of water…just like our lives full of burdens.) Rowing a canoe in itself is extremely strenuous if you do not exercise and you find muscles that you never knew you had. (They let you know where they are through pain!) It had also been extremely dry, so we often had to stop and carry our canoe over the dry places. (We often try to carry our burdens all alone but God wants to carry them for us.)

It was a very long day and when I found out we were only half way to our ending point, I was ready to quit. I actually told the other chaperone to just go to the bank and leave me there. I thought that I would just walk up in the woods there and die because I simply did not have the energy to keep going. Of course, I was being a little dramatic and I "bucked up" and completed the trip. (I will not be signing up to chaperone that trip again! OK. I know. I should never tell God what I am not going to do.)

That canoe trip is a lot like life. Sometimes we feel like life is just so overwhelming that we want to give up. We just feel like there is no possible way to keep going. The fact is that life is hard. There are many struggles in life and we actually bring some of them on ourselves! But there is hope. God has all of the answers and He is always there for us.

You can have total and complete freedom, even in the midst of trials, if you will totally and completely put your trust in God. God alone is the answer to each and every problem that we face. He alone can provide the peace that we are all searching for within our hearts. I pray that God will use this book to draw you to Him, where He can provide you comfort and rest through it all. Give it all to God and you will be amazed at the transformation that will take place within you.

I am writing this book with a humble heart and I pray that God will use the sharing of my trials to help others. I have daily struggles but even in the midst of my trials, God has given me a peace and freedom that I cannot explain. I want to give God the full glory that He deserves. I am just a plain, ordinary person on the outside; however, God is doing an extraordinary work within me.

We all have some kind of problems, troubles, sorrow, and heartache. I pray that my honesty in this book will help others who are struggling. If sharing my story will help just one person, this book will have been worth writing. I will stop now and tell you that this has not been easy and I have cried more tears than I ever thought imaginable but God has used my struggles to make me into who He wants me to be. Psalm 56:8 says "Thou tellest my wanderings: put thou my tears into thy bottle: are they not in thy book?" (KJV) Wow! God has all of our tears in a bottle. (It's a huge bottle to hold my tears!) He loves us that much! How can we not totally surrender to Him? Of course, He will be working on me until I get to heaven because none of us ever reach perfection on earth. Jesus was the only perfect one to walk this earth.

I am currently going through an extremely painful time in my life but God is with me, carrying me, through it all. I can honestly say that I have no regrets at all because God has used every single situation to teach me and mold me. I do have many friends that have gone through this and I hope that by sharing my story, God's grace will be revealed to others who are going through various life struggles. Please, do not judge me or my husband after reading this story. We must leave the judging to God. Romans 14:10-13 says, "You, then, why do you judge your brother? Or why do you look down on your brother? For we will all stand before God's judgment seat. It is written: 'As surely as I live,' says the Lord, 'every knee will bow before me; every tongue will confess to God.' So then, each of us will give an account of himself to God. Therefore let us stop passing judgment on one another. Instead, make up your mind not to put any stumbling block or obstacle in your brother's way."

I give God the glory for everything in my life. I praise Him in the midst of the storm because He is in control. Although I am facing a pending divorce, it is only by God's grace and mercy that my divorce is not already final. Had Wendy been in control, my divorce would have been final months ago and I would be filled with bitterness, anger, and hatred. I have made such a mess but God will take all of my mess and make something glorious. Hebrews 11:1 tells us, "Now faith is being sure of what we hope for and certain of what we do not see."

I can assure you that if you will totally surrender to God, He will transform your life beyond imagination. Please allow God to speak to you as you read this book. God has totally and completely transformed me and the transformation continues. I awaken every single morning thinking that there is no possible way to be any closer to Him, however, He draws me closer and provides more and more strength each and every day. I pray that you will allow Him to transform you as well. God not only gives us strength to endure trials, but He can use every single trial to help someone else if we will open up our hearts and lives to others.

Dedication

This book is dedicated to my Lord and Savior. I continue to be awestruck daily by His loving presence and amazing grace and mercy in my life. I also want to thank Him for blessing me with 2 wonderful sons, Austin and Hayden, and my husband.

Contents:

Chapter 1:

Why do we hide our trials and troubles?

❦

On November 14, 2008 (the day after my birthday), my husband, Dennis, nonchalantly told me while standing in the kitchen with our kids in the next room that he had committed adultery. He refused to tell me much because he was "protecting" the other woman. He also could not assure me that it was over. I had always said since I was a teenager that if anyone ever cheated on me, that would be it. Well, you've heard the old saying "never say never." You see, that very day on my way home from work, I had prayed for God to give me a sign that I was where He wanted me to be in life. Just moments after I prayed that prayer, God revealed to me the most beautiful rainbow that I had ever seen in my life.

I automatically thought of that rainbow as I stood speechless in the kitchen. Next, God brought to mind my Sunday School lesson. I teach a Ladies Sunday School class and our lesson for the month of November was on forgiveness. (You know those lessons are planned in advance and this was all part of God's perfect timing. Our class is the only class in the church to use this literature and the topics had been right on target for our class participants for years. That is how God works.)

Dennis belittled me and blamed me for the adultery. (He refused to call it an affair and I went along with this.) Dennis had already packed a bag and told me he was going to stay at a friend's house. I told him not to leave. I told him that I forgave him and we could work this out. He went to bed while I stayed up the entire night crying, praying and reading the Bible. God led me to the book of Hosea during the night. I awakened Dennis and on my knees, I apologized for not being the wife that I should have been and I begged him to reconcile our marriage. His response was very cold and he went back to sleep. The next day, he continued to blame me for our horrible marriage. Once again, I stayed up all night crying and praying and reading the Bible.

After 2 nights of no sleep and not eating, I felt God telling me that I needed to ask Dennis to move out. I went to Dennis' work on that Sunday morning before church and I asked him to move out. His response was "so this is how it's going to be." His girlfriend was there with him at the time, flaunting herself in front of me. I then went on to church to teach the Sunday School class about forgiveness. (Only through God's strength was that possible!)

I continued for weeks to believe Dennis that it was all my fault and I repeatedly begged him to work on our marriage. I repeatedly received a cold response that I had a chance for 17 years to work on things and I had failed. I literally wasted away during these weeks as I lost down to 98 pounds. God, in His infinite wisdom, during one of those many sleepless nights, led me to 2 Corinthians 4:16-18, "Therefore we do not lose heart. Though outwardly we are wasting away, yet inwardly we are being renewed day by day. For our light and momentary troubles are achieving for us an eternal glory that far outweighs them all. So we fix our eyes not on what is seen, but on what is unseen. For what is seen is temporary, but what is unseen is eternal."

I could not continue to live like this as I had 2 sons that needed me. I finally was able to break free from this bondage of believing the lie that it was my fault. After all, I was just as miserable in the marriage as he was, if not more so, and I did not choose to have an affair. Life is all about choices.

I also had the mindset that God could use this to help others. I was trying to think of ways that God could use me through this. Now, God could use this for His glory. The problem was that I was trying to use it for His glory without His guidance. I guess that I was actually acting as a martyr. My dad is a very respectable Christian and I explained to him that if my story could save just one other marriage from going through adultery, then it was worth the sacrifice. (That was only 4 days after Dennis told me of the affair.) My dad quickly told me that I could not do that. I did not listen and went on thinking that I could use this situation for God's glory. I had an attitude to be a "self-sacrifice" as Jesus was a sacrifice. Again, I was wrong!

God has provided me with His strength throughout this whole ordeal. However, I did do many things on my own, thinking that it was the "Christian thing to do." I made the situation much worse because I did not totally listen to what God was telling me to do. I ended up having health problems due to stress. God can and will use this situation for His glory but it has to be His plan and in His timing.

Let me stop now and say adultery is a sin and there is never a reason or excuse to commit adultery. God's Word tells us that, as Christians, our bodies are not our own. We are His temple because He lives inside of us. 1 Corinthians 6:19-20 tells us, "Do you not know that your body is a temple of the Holy Spirit, who is in you, whom you have received from God? You are not your own; you were bought at a price. Therefore honor God with your body."

We give our bodies to whomever we have sex with and there are numerous repercussions. One of the many consequences is sexually transmitted diseases (STD) that are rampant these days. We not only are subjecting ourselves to STDs but we are also spreading these to our spouses, whom we supposedly love and cherish. We violate our own bodies and our spouse's body when we commit adultery. We violate our marriage vows that we made to our spouse and to God. If you are considering having an affair, please run the other way as fast as you can. The momentary pleasure that you may have is not worth the pain that you will cause to yourself, your spouse, lover and the families that you will destroy.

Satan is definitely attacking marriages. I do not care how miserable you are in your marriage. An affair is not the answer. You can avoid the temptation by never allowing yourself to be in a situation alone with the opposite sex. Do not discuss marital problems with the opposite sex. Do not even allow that door to open. You have that choice to make. 1 Corinthians 10:13 tells us, "No temptation has seized you except what is common to man. And God is faithful; He will not let you be tempted beyond what you can bear. But when you are tempted, He will also provide a way out so that you can stand up under it."

Although the "grass may look greener on the other side", it turns brown after you get there. Remember, looks can be deceiving. Hebrews 13:4 says, "Marriage should be honored by all, and the marriage bed kept pure, for God will judge the adulterer and all the sexually immoral." If you have justified having an affair, Satan has deceived you. However, it is never too late. If you repent and turn to God, He is just and He will forgive. 1 John 1:9 tells us, "If we confess our sins, He is faithful and just and will forgive us our sins and purify us from all unrighteousness."

Adultery is too common in today's society. Years ago after I began an employment, I was told by a female co-worker that I barely knew that she needed to speak with me in private. I went to speak with her and she asked, "I know you are married but are you happily married?" I asked why she was asking me that question. (Thankfully, I did not answer her in that I was miserable in my marriage at that time.) She explained that one of our male co-workers was interested in me and she was trying to set us up. I immediately told her that I was happily married and that I was not interested. (OK. I lied about the happily married but I was totally shocked and needed to leave. I just justified a lie. We'll talk more about how we are not to lie in another chapter.) Now, is that really what our world has come to? We have people who are trying to set up married people to commit adultery. Really, what does "happily" have anything to do with it? If we are married, that should be final. We are committed to one spouse for the rest of our lives.

1 Corinthians 7:17 says, "And don't be wishing you were someplace else or with someone else. Where you are right now is God's place for you. Live and obey and love and believe right there. God, not your marital status, defines your life. Don't think I'm being harder on you than on the others. I give this same counsel in all the churches." (MSG)

Several weeks after Dennis told me about the affair, I was given a wonderful Bible Study to help me through. I immediately started on the Bible Study and it helped me tremendously. I felt God telling me to facilitate this Bible Study at my church. I immediately began seeking others at my church that may have already done that study and would be willing to teach it. After all, I was in the midst of my struggles and I did not think it possible for me to lead that study without crying throughout it. I also thought that certainly there were others who were wiser than me and more equipped to lead the Bible Study. (Once again, I justified trying to do things my way instead of God's way.) Well, God wanted me to facilitate it and He provided me with the strength to do it.

I wish that I could say that I always automatically do what God tells me but the truth is that I often try to do things my way first.

God had also heavily burdened my heart over broken marriages and families 3 weeks prior to Dennis' admission. Our Sunday School class had started meeting during the week to pray specifically for marriages and families as we saw Satan attacking marriages all around us. I have always been against divorce. I know that God hates divorce and therefore, I hate divorce. However, I felt God leading me to go file for divorce. I know this sounds crazy but I could not remain married to Dennis while he was continuing in an affair with no intention of stopping the affair.

Matthew 19:3-12 tells us the following about divorce, "Some Pharisees came to him to test him. They asked, 'Is it lawful for a man to divorce his wife for any and every reason? Haven't you read,' He replied, 'that at the beginning the Creator made them male and female', and said, 'For this reason a man will leave his father and mother and be united to his wife, and the two will become one flesh?' So they are no longer two, but one. Therefore what God has joined together, let man not separate.' 'Why then', they asked, 'did Moses command that a man give his wife a certificate of divorce and send her away?' Jesus replied, 'Moses permitted you to divorce your wives because your hearts were hard. But it was not this way from the beginning. I tell you that anyone who divorces his wife, except for marital unfaithfulness, and marries another woman commits adultery.' The disciples said to Him, 'If this is the situation between a husband and wife, it is better not to marry.' Jesus replied, 'Not everyone can accept this word, but only those to whom it has been given. For some are eunuchs because they were born that way; others were made that way by men; and others have renounced marriage because of the kingdom of heaven. The one who can accept this should accept it.'"

With a heavy heart, although I knew this was what God was leading me to do, I scheduled an appointment and met with the attorney. That night, I told Dennis that I had met with the attorney and I was filing for divorce. The day before, Dennis had told me that he wanted a divorce; however, he wanted to just sit down and divide things how he thought they should be divided. I wanted to divide things in half to be "fair." (Like any of this whole situation was "fair.") I wanted to see an attorney to make sure that I was covering the legal basis and that the finances were handled fairly. I honestly believe that Dennis would have been perfectly fine with the divorce had he been able to take what he wanted at that time.

After I told Dennis that I had met with the attorney, Dennis told me that he did not want a divorce. I accused him of only wanting the marriage due to financial reasons. I knew that God hates divorce so I wanted to believe that we would not get a divorce but I still felt led to continue with the divorce proceedings and the divorce papers were filed. Of course, Dennis asked that he not be served the papers at work and I agreed for him to go to the attorney's office to receive the papers. I did not realize at the time that he was still in the affair. I was told by many that I was being too nice and I should have had Dennis and the other woman served.

We have gone through months of attempting at reconciliation and I will discuss this throughout the book. The emotions have been absolutely overwhelming at times but I have finally learned to allow God to have my crazy emotions and He has provided me with an indescribable peace even in the midst of the pending divorce. God also convicted me that although I was accusing Dennis of only wanting the marriage due to financial reasons, maybe that was why I was holding on. I had left my employment that I depended on to support my family only 3 months prior to Dennis' affair. If I still had that employment, I would have been financially independent but at this moment, I needed Dennis' income to support the family. I was angry that this was happening. I had been financially independent for so many years and I felt so taken advantage of that I wanted to make it right. I wanted to stand up and get what I felt I deserved.

Speaking of "deserved", no, I did not deserve for Dennis to have an affair and no, Dennis did not deserve to have another chance with me. (I will not mention just how many chances there have been at this point because I lost count months ago.) God again gave me a reality check. Did Jesus deserve to live in this cruel, harsh world and be crucified on the cross for me? I do not deserve Jesus' love and grace and mercy. I am a sinner. Jesus was without sin. Jesus knew what was going to happen to Him and He chose to come to earth anyway because He loves you and me that much. So, let's get off the high horse about "deserving" things and having our "rights being violated".

It took months for God to finally get through to me that I was not being dependent upon God for my financial future. God will provide for my every need. This includes finances. I was still thinking that I needed to provide for my family and I was not giving this part to God. God wants our total and complete dependence on Him. We live from paycheck to paycheck and this is with both of our incomes. How could we possibly make it living separately? I was living in fear of not being able to pay bills. Where was my faith? I was talking about faith to everyone and sharing my faith about other areas of my life but I did not have faith in this area. I had actually quit my other job by stepping out in faith that God would provide so why didn't I believe that now? Only 3 months had passed since I had totally believed that God would provide for our finances and now I was living in fear.

The truth is that material possessions will all pass away. We are to store up our treasures in Heaven. Matthew 6:19-20 tells us, "Do not store up for yourselves treasures on earth, where moth and rust destroy, and where thieves break in and steal. But store up for yourselves treasures in heaven, where moth and rust do not destroy, and where thieves do not break in and steal."

I finally surrendered my financial concerns to God and I know without a doubt that He will provide. I honestly am not worried about my financial future and I have let go of my "I deserve half" attitude. I know God will provide no matter what the outcome.

God also revealed that I had a negative attitude about divorce. I honestly never thought that I would be divorced. (I realize that sounds arrogant and God has definitely humbled me through this.) Although God hates divorce, God does allow us to make choices and both partners do not always make the choice to follow God's good and perfect will for our lives. I must stay focused on God and what God wants for my life and God will take care of everything else. I will turn 40 in a few months and it appears that I will be divorced in a few months. In the past I thought that sounded depressing; however, I know without a doubt that God has a good and perfect plan for my life and His plan will prevail. I do not need to hold on to anything on this earth. I need to keep focused on Him and Him alone.

I was raised, as many of my generation, to keep my personal problems to myself. I realize writing a book about my problems is going against what I was taught. I do not agree that we should keep our problems to ourselves. There are so many hurting people out there that honestly believe they are all alone. We do not know what others are going through because we do not share. We have family members, friends, and neighbors who have all gone through some of our same problems and we could help each other tremendously if we would only share.

Some of us like to share our problems, however, many of us tend to keep our problems to ourselves. Pride is often the cause of us not wanting to share our hurts. We think if our image does not appear tarnished, then we are doing great. This is such a lie and it is straight from Satan. If Satan can keep us quiet and continue feeding us lies, then he will eventually have us so hardened that we no longer can even recognize the truth. The truth, God's Word, really will set you free. Satan is the father of lies while God is the father of truth. John 8:44-45 says, "You belong to your father, the devil, and you want to carry out your father's desire. He was a murderer from the beginning, not holding to the truth, for there is no truth in him. When he lies, he speaks his native language, for he is a liar and the father of lies. Yet because I tell the truth, you do not believe me!" Keeping our feelings inside will give Satan a chance to get into our thoughts and deceive us. He does this gradually and then he has a stronghold over us and we do not even know that we have been deceived. He is a sneaky devil.

Galatians 6:7-10 tells us, "Do not be deceived: God cannot be mocked. A man reaps what he sows. The one who sows to please his sinful nature, from that nature will reap destruction; the one who sows to please the Spirit, from the Spirit will reap eternal life. Let us not become weary in doing good, for at the proper time we will reap a harvest if we do not give up. Therefore, as we have opportunity, let us do good to all people, especially to those who belong to the family of believers."

I realize the truth in our lives is not always easy to accept but we are not guaranteed an easy life. The Bible tells us that we will face troubles. James 1: 2 says "Consider it pure joy, my brothers, whenever you face trials of many kinds". Notice this says "whenever" not "if". We will face heartache and troubles in this life; however, we are not alone. God is always with us and He will never leave us or forsake us. Hebrews 13:5 says, "Keep your lives free from the love of money and be content with what you have, because God has said, 'Never will I leave you; never will I forsake you.'"

Although God already knows our thoughts, He wants us to voice them to Him. He wants to have a relationship with us. He wants us to give Him all of our burdens and He will give us rest. Matthew 11:28-30 says, "Come to me, all you who are weary and burdened, and I will give you rest. Take my yoke upon you and learn from me, for I am gentle and humble in heart, and you will find rest for your souls. For my yoke is easy and my burden is light."

He also provides other Christians so we can fellowship with them. We are never alone. God's Word tells us that we are to help others. Hebrews 3:12-13 says, "See to it, brothers, that none of you has a sinful, unbelieving heart that turns away from the living God. But encourage one another daily, as long as it is called today, so that none of you may be hardened by sin's deceitfulness." I believe that God allows us to go through trials and tribulations to mold us into His image, to increase our faith and to help others who go through our similar circumstances. I believe that we should change the old saying "when life gives you lemons...make lemonade" to when life gives you lemons...give it to God and He will make much more than lemonade.

We all have problems. I was reared in the Baptist church and it still amazes me how people want to hide their "skeletons" in the closet and never discuss them. There are so many who have mental illnesses, depression, family members who are homosexuals, family members who have addictions or are in prison. Why would we try to hide this from our own church family? There is freedom in getting it all out and not trying to hide anything. I can tell you that secrets and lies can cause physical problems in addition to the anger and bitterness that builds with every secret and lie that you hold inside.

There are so many people who have depression and choose to suffer alone. This is an illness just like any physical illness. Depression is not something to be ashamed of. God is the Great Physician and He can heal you. However,

He also provided us with doctors. There is medication and therapy available for depression. I am not saying that everyone should be medicated but sometimes we do need medication. Sometimes we go through seasons in our life where we need an anti-depressant and sometimes we need them long-term. If you feel you are depressed, please talk with your physician. Now, I will tell you that there are many counselors out there that will give you "worldly advice." If you do need counseling, seek a Christian counselor.

Some people who become depressed just cannot see any way out of their troubles and they think of suicide. Suicide is never the answer. It does not matter what has happened to you or what you have done. God loves you more than you can imagine. You are special to God and He created each and every one of us to be on this earth for a reason. God wants to heal you and He is right there with you if you will only seek Him.

If you are thinking of suicide, please seek help from your doctor, counselor, pastor, friend, or family member immediately. Let me say again that suicide is never the answer. When I was completing my internship, I had a fellow student tell me that everyone had contemplated suicide at some time in their life. Well, I was in my early 20's and I had never thought of suicide but I thought I was just naïve. So, as we discussed this with our instructor, she thought that I was crazy because I simply repeated what the other student had said. My instructor quickly informed me that thinking of suicide is not normal. (Do you see how easily we are swayed into thinking as the world thinks?) I knew that this was not normal but I did not want to appear different. I now realize that being different is a good thing if we are standing out for God.

I know some people who are so private (that's the nice word for secretive) that they do not even share with their own family members. Some of us were taught to be private. No,

I am not blaming our parents for anything. I just think that it is time to break this cycle. There are many who refuse to share anything personal with anyone. They only have casual relationships for fear someone may find out about their past. We all have a past. We cannot heal by burying it deep within and fearing that someone may find out about it. Hiding our past hurts only hinders our growth in God. To be totally and completely healed, we must give God all of the pieces and allow His transforming Grace to restore us.

I have facilitated many groups and asked the members to share their experiences. I cannot tell you how many times people have approached me after group and told me that they felt so much better hearing other people's issues. They admitted that their problems did not seem near as bad as the next person. So often we get consumed with our own situations and we cannot see beyond ourselves. This is another way Satan works. We then become self-centered and hardened. Hebrews 3:15 tells us, "As has just been said: 'Today, if you hear his voice, do not harden your hearts as you did in the rebellion.'" If we would only open up to others and listen to them and share. There is actually healing in helping others. When we help others we often turn our focus away from our own problems.

God does not want us to keep everything to ourselves. Matthew 11:28-30 says, "Come to me, all you who are weary and burdened, and I will give you rest. Take my yoke upon you and learn from me, for I am gentle and humble in heart, and you will find rest for your souls. For my yoke is easy and my burden is light." Bring all of your sorrow, burdens, and heartaches straight to Him and He will give you rest.

He wants us to learn from our trials and use them to help others. His Word tells us that Christian fellowship is vital. Hebrews 10:23-24 says, "Let us hold unswervingly to the hope we profess, for he who promised is faithful. And let us consider how we may spur one another on toward love and good deeds." Satan seeks to alienate and destroy us. We cannot allow Satan to draw us in to his deceitful schemes. We must take a stand and share with other Christians as God has called us to do. Lamentations 1:16 says, "This is why I weep and my eyes overflow with tears. No one is near to comfort me, no one to restore my spirit. My children are destitute because the enemy has prevailed."

Why do we fear what other people think? As Christians, we should only care what God thinks. I know that this is easier said than done but it can be done with God. God is the only One that we should fear. I experienced struggles my entire life to try to please everyone. This has led to constant frustration because pleasing everyone is humanly impossible. We are called to please God and God alone. As I am writing this book, I began fearing what my family and friends will say. I cannot write this book as God is leading me to without being totally honest and sharing from my heart. However, there are certain things that I will not be able to share out of respect for my family.

There is so much hurt and pain but yet we dress up on Sunday mornings and "put on our happy face" to go to church. Some examples of those hurting are loss of family or friends, wayward children, divorce, incest, abuse, addictions, depression, and marital/family discord. The list is endless. The church is God's home and its members are His body. We are family. Why do we try to hide what is going on in our lives from our church family? If each of us would open up and share, we would realize that we all have problems. God will use you to help someone else. Helping others will help to get our focus off of our own problems.

Chapter 2:

Who are we here to serve and please?

Who are you serving? We are called to serve God and God alone. It took me years to realize this but if we put our spouse in front of God, then we are serving our spouse. If we put our children or anyone above God, we are not serving God. God belongs first in our lives. It is that simple. Romans 8:6-8 tells us, "The mind of sinful man is death, but the mind controlled by the Spirit is life and peace; the sinful mind is hostile to God. It does not submit to God's law, nor can it do so. Those controlled by the sinful nature cannot please God."

Matthew 6:24 says, "No one can serve two masters. Either he will hate the one and love the other, or he will be devoted to the one and despise the other. You cannot serve both God and money." This scripture is very clear that we cannot serve 2 masters and there is no middle ground. Revelation 3:15-16 tells us, "I know your deeds, that you are neither cold nor hot. I wish you were either one or the other! So, because you are lukewarm—neither hot nor cold—I am about to spit you out of my mouth."

I spent many years trying to please everyone around me. I did not really see anything wrong with this. It was just my personality and I thought I was being nice to everyone and I was doing what God wanted. Boy, did I have a wakeup call! I could not please everyone and that troubled me greatly. We cannot allow our words and actions to be dictated by man. We must allow God's Word to flow through us. Galatians 1:10 says, "Am I now trying to win the approval of men, or of God? Or am I trying to please men? If I were still trying to please men, I would not be a servant of Christ."

For many years of our marriage, I tried everything that I could to please Dennis, to no avail. I ended up extremely frustrated. I thought I was a failure because I could not even please my own husband. After many years, I finally quit trying to please him and I began to grow resentful and bitter toward him. Our marriage was absolutely miserable and we barely even knew each other. The only time we ever went anywhere together was to ride to church together on Sunday mornings. Of course, we put on our happy faces!

God has recently revealed to me that I went about the whole process wrong. Once again, I thought I knew best and tried it my way which only ended in misery. I am not going to say "if only" because I would not have the relationship with God that I have today if I had not been drug through the trenches. Ok, not really drug. God carried me the whole time! I am not on this earth to try to please Dennis or anyone else. I am on this earth to please God and God alone. If I truly seek God with all of my heart and soul, He will guide me and bless me beyond measure. Don't get me wrong here, we are called to be submissive to our husbands but we are not to put our husbands above God. The man is the head of the household but God is to be head of man.

Now this blessing beyond measure may not be on this side of heaven. Oh, but the glorious riches we will receive in heaven. You see, our circumstances on earth will change but God never changes. He is omnipresent, omnipotent and omniscience. He is the Alpha and Omega. He is the Great I Am. If we can only learn to keep our focus on Him every second of every day, we will experience His true joy. However, the second that we look at our circumstances, Satan starts working overtime to keep our focus away from our Heavenly Father.

While we were supposedly trying to reconcile, Dennis continued the affair and the lying. I tried to have him "prove his love for me" by calling me throughout the day, meeting with our pastor, having 2 accountability partners who were deacons, going to counseling, and reading a book. Of course, this failed also. He refused to do what I requested and he selected which of the things he would half-heartedly do. I felt God telling me to let Dennis go because God wanted his undivided attention. And I did let him go, several times. But every time I let him go, He did not appear to turn to God. So, I felt I needed to work on him some more because surely God needed my assistance. Wrong! Remember, God does not need us! I will go ahead and tell you upfront. I made a huge mess, although my intentions were good. I was not listening to God.

I still feel that we need to work through all of our issues together; however, Dennis wants to forget about it and move on. I know that history repeats itself if we do not learn from our mistakes and I want to work through all of the problems to prevent this from occurring again. Dennis said that anytime that I brought it up, I was being negative and he did not need to be around a negative attitude. I was still trying to make the marriage work so I went along with this. I kept everything buried while it was killing me on the inside.

If we have a spider bite and it gets infected, do we just put a band-aid over it and hope that it goes away? I am sorry but the infection just grows under the band-aid and it does not go away without treatment. It becomes painful and we eventually must seek medical attention. The treatment is usually to remove the core of the infection and antibiotics. This is the same with sin. If we try to bury it without addressing the core of the problem, the core grows and hardens our hearts. We must seek the Great Physician to remove the core of the sin problem and allow Him to treat us and make us whole and complete in Him. We cannot conquer sin alone nor do we have to. Jesus has already paid the price for our sins and He will forgive our sins if we confess and repent. Now, true repentance means that we do not continue in the sin.

Satan wants us to keep everything inside so he can control our thoughts and emotions. God's Word tells us to shed light on the sin and repent. Ephesians 5:11-14 says, "Have nothing to do with the fruitless deeds of darkness, but rather expose them. For it is shameful even to mention what the disobedient do in secret. But everything exposed by the light becomes visible, for it is light that makes everything visible. This is why it is said: 'Wake up, O sleeper, rise from the dead, and Christ will shine on you.'" 1 Corinthians 4:5 tells us, "Therefore judge nothing before the appointed time; wait till the Lord comes. He will bring to light what is hidden in darkness and will expose the motives of men's hearts. At that time each will receive his praise from God." We cannot hide our sin or cover up our sin. God knows everything!

If we allow Satan to control our thoughts and our hearts, we eventually become so hardened that we do not ever turn back to God. Ephesians 4:18-19 says, "They are darkened in their understanding and separated from the life of God because of the ignorance that is in them due to the hardening of their hearts. Having lost all sensitivity, they have given themselves over to sensuality so as to indulge in every kind of impurity, with a continual lust for more." When this happens, we lead a lonely, miserable life constantly in search for things that we never find.

Satan does not have your best interest in mind. He seeks to kill and destroy. John 10:9-11 says, "I am the gate; whoever enters through me will be saved. He will come in and go out, and find pasture. The thief comes only to steal and kill and destroy; I have come that they may have life and have it to the full. I am the good shepherd. The good shepherd lays down his life for the sheep." Are the momentary pleasures of this world really worth eternity in hell?

I thought that Dennis and I were managing to hide most of our marital problems from our children. Once again, I was wrong. I wanted to make sure that our sons were ok and I would ask them every night if there was anything they wanted to talk about. One night, my 14 year old son began asking me questions. I was very guarded and he picked up on this right away. He looked me dead in the eye and asked "Mom, he's not here, why are you still allowing him to control you?" How could this 14 year old child have more insight than me? Did I really want my children to grow up believing that it is ok to be controlled by someone or to control someone?

I finally realized that I had been under Dennis' control for our entire marriage. I have a Master's degree in Social Work and I have been a counselor for years. I knew all of the signs but I never saw it in my own marriage. I am not trying to sound like a saint or anything because believe me, Dennis has made it very clear that my OCD personality has been beyond difficult to live with. I have my own controlling issues. Well, I did. I can honestly say that I have given those to God now. It was a struggle, but I finally let go. I used to like to be organized and I wanted everything to work out exactly how I thought it should be. (Could you imagine living with someone like that?)

I just could not believe that I was so quick to pick up the controlling spouse signs in others but I never saw it in my own home. This is an example of how we accept and mask things right under our own roofs to keep from dealing with it. We were not created to be controlled by anyone but God. For all of those years, although I was blinded to it, I was allowing Dennis to control me over my Lord and Savior. This was not Dennis' fault. I allowed it to happen probably to try to please him since I had that pleasing personality. (There I go with excuses!)

Now that I have acknowledged the problem, I must surrender it totally and completely to God for Him to free me from this control. I still have the nature to want to please which causes me to easily fall under that control and not voice the truth for fear of hurting Dennis' feelings or making him mad. I cannot live in fear. I must allow God to totally free me from this. God will free me from this as long as I surrender it to Him and quit trying to take it back. I still kind of struggle with not wanting to speak the truth to Dennis but God is immediately bringing this to my attention and God will not allow me to do anything until I discuss what is bothering me with Dennis.

We also must be very careful that we are not looking to our spouse to love us in a way that only God can love us. Yes, the husband is called to love his wife as Christ loved the church. Ephesians 5:25 says, "Husbands, love your wives, just as Christ loved the church and gave himself up for her." However, we cannot depend on our spouses to fill a void that only God can fill. We cannot expect a human to give us what only God can provide.

During our period of trying to reconcile, I tried to change everything possible that Dennis wanted me to change. I was trying to prove to him that I could change and I believed that if I changed, Dennis would want me instead of other women. I know many others who have tried to change "to win their cheating spouse back". This is like we are agreeing with our spouse that we were the reason that they had an affair and we will change if they will come back to us. After months, I finally realized that it did not matter what I changed. I was not the problem. I needed to stay focused on God and only change things that God revealed to me to change. I did not need to compete with the "other woman". I was created in God's image and I needed to be who God created me to be and not who I thought that Dennis wanted me to be.

Cheating spouses choose to have an affair because of sin. It is not the faithful spouse's fault. The cheating spouse tries to justify their actions and blame the other to ease their guilt. The cheating spouse actually begins to believe these lies about their faithful spouse. That is how Satan works. Satan will even try to get the faithful spouse to have an affair out of revenge. Satan justifies this in making us believe that our cheating spouse deserves to feel the pain that we feel. The faithful spouse can not fall into this trap. The faithful spouse must turn to God for all answers.

Why do we want to remain married to a cheating spouse anyway? That was always my attitude before it happened to me. I always thought that if they cheated once, they could never be trusted. The truth is that if they have a truly repentant heart, God will change them. God knows all of our hearts and our trust and faith is in God. If God joined you together and you are both faithful to Him, God will reconcile the marriage and make it what a marriage is supposed to be.

What kind of twisted mind games do we play with our spouses? If he comes in late from work, then we "play the quiet game." If she does not have dinner cooked on time, he blows up and throws a fit. If he does not pick up the kids on time, she gets angry and lets it build up and fester inside so it will come out later all at one time. If she does not have his work pants clean when he is getting dressed for work, he gets furious. If he buys a boat without her knowledge, she retaliates by going on a shopping spree. If she does not tell him that she loves him then he does not tell her. Is your love really so shallow that it is based only if they love you? Ok, you get the picture. We act like children. Instead of discussing things like civil adults, we play mind games with each other. We must quit playing games and be totally honest with our spouse, family and friends.

Married couples should work together. Ephesians 6:7-8 says, "Serve wholeheartedly, as if you were serving the Lord, not men, because you know that the Lord will reward everyone for whatever good he does, whether he is slave or free." We should truly be soul mates with each other. (Did you roll your eyes at that?) It's true. We made a commitment before our Lord to obey, honor and cherish till death do us part. (That's not giving anyone consent to go kill their mate to get out of their commitment.) Where are our morals and standards? Why do we so readily "throw in the towel" when things do not go our way? We truly need to evaluate our own morals and ethics and commitments. I believe the Christians have blended in with the rest of the world because we do not stand for anything. We make up excuses for everything. If someone chooses to have an affair, we turn our heads and say "everybody else is doing it." Does that make it right? Think about what our parents always asked us, "If they jumped off the bridge, would you jump too?"

Let's get real. We need to quit playing games and be who God has called us to be. We must swallow our pride and allow God to break down those barriers. We can truly love our spouse and feel free around him/her. We must focus on God's way instead of our way or their way. Satan fell from Heaven due to pride and he uses pride to cause us to fall. What if each of us loved our spouse as instructed in the Bible. 1 Corinthians 13:4-8a says, "Love is patient, love is kind. It does not envy, it does not boast, it is not proud. It is not rude, it is not self-seeking, it is not easily angered, it keeps no record of wrongs. Love does not delight in evil but rejoices with the truth. It always protects, always trusts, always hopes, always perseveres. Love never fails..." Please read through those verses again and ask God to reveal to you if you need to change the way that you love your spouse, family member, friend, or co-worker.

There is so much pain in the world today. Family members and friends hurt each other. We have incest, child molestation, rape, and many other atrocious crimes. 2 Timothy 3:1-5 tells us, "But mark this: There will be terrible times in the last days. People will be lovers of themselves, lovers of money, boastful, proud, abusive, disobedient to their parents, ungrateful, unholy, without love, unforgiving, slanderous, without self-control, brutal, not lovers of the good, treacherous, rash, conceited, lovers of pleasure rather than lovers of God— having a form of godliness but denying its power. Have nothing to do with them." We need to allow God to search us and reveal to us if any of this is referring to us. Remember, we all think that it is the other person's fault. We are the other person. If you really look at these verses, it perfectly describes our current world.

We need each other. We need to allow God to tear down the barriers and remove the masks. We need to care about each other. We need to let Jesus live through us. Just imagine how much easier it would be to face negative circumstances if you and your spouse were truly one as the Bible describes husbands and wives.

Think about it, most Christians actually want to blend in with the world for various reasons. Some think that the world seems like more fun. I can assure you that hell will not be more fun than heaven. I can also assure you that one day every knee will bow and every tongue will confess that Jesus Christ is Lord. Philippians 2:10-11 tells us, "that at the name of Jesus every knee should bow, in heaven and on earth and under the earth, and every tongue confess that Jesus Christ is Lord, to the glory of God the Father." Since you are going to confess Jesus Christ is Lord in the end, why not choose to follow him now? Don't you want to hear "Well done my good and faithful servant"? Jesus Christ has already won the battle. He has already defeated Satan and death. Do you want to be on the winning team? John 12:31 tells us, "Now is the time for judgment on this world; now the prince of this world will be driven out." Who are you choosing to follow right now?

I joined the church and was baptized when I was 9 years old. I actually became a Christian earlier but my parents wanted to make sure that I understood what I was doing so I waited until I was 9 to make the decision public. I remember the day after my Baptism; I went to school wanting to change the whole world. I wanted everyone to know that I was a Christian and I wanted the whole world to have what I had. I wish that I could say that I kept that attitude throughout my life. The truth is that I went through times that I wanted to fit in with the world. I did not want to stand out because that drew attention to me and I did not want any attention. Blending in was so much easier. We are not called to take the easy way or to blend in!

Although I was a Christian, I went through many years of doubting my salvation. I was constantly seeking assurance. I feared God and I wanted to be certain that I did not go to hell. I mean, was it really that easy? Could I really be saved for all of eternity just by saying a simple prayer? Yes, it really is that easy. John 5:11-13 says, "And this is the testimony: God has given us eternal life, and this life is in his Son. He who has the Son has life; he who does not have the Son of God does not have life. I write these things to you who believe in the name of the Son of God so that you may know that you have eternal life." However, if we truly ask Jesus to live in our heart then we die to ourselves and live for Him. I believe our churches are full of people who honestly believe that they are Christians but they do not have Jesus living in them. I know, only God knows the heart and only God knows who has salvation. Matthew 7:1-2 says, "Do not judge, or you too will be judged. For in the same way you judge others, you will be judged, and with the measure you use, it will be measured to you."

Is Jesus living through you? Do your family, friends, and co-workers see Jesus living through you or do you leave Jesus at church on Sundays? I challenge you to ask those who spend the most time with you to honestly tell you if they see Jesus living through you. Be open and not defensive of their responses. Allow God to transform you.

2 Corinthians 5:17 says, "Therefore, if anyone is in Christ, he is a new creation; the old has gone, the new has come!" Colossians 2:6 tells us, "So then, just as you received Christ Jesus as Lord, continue to live in him." Titus 1:16 says, "They claim to know God, but by their actions they deny him. They are detestable, disobedient and unfit for doing anything good."

The fact is that some people claim to know God but they actually do not. Even Satan believes in God and Satan knows scripture. Sadly, Satan knows scripture better than some Christians and he uses this to deceive us. 2 Corinthians 11:14-15 tells us, "And no wonder, for Satan himself masquerades as an angel of light. It is not surprising, then, if his servants masquerade as servants of righteousness. Their end will be what their actions deserve." Are you certain without a shadow of a doubt that if you were to die today that you would go to heaven? This is the most important decision that you will ever make in your entire life.

Romans 8:6 says, "The mind of sinful man is death, but the mind controlled by the Spirit is life and peace." Romans 8:13 says, "For if you live according to the sinful nature, you will die; but if by the Spirit you put to death the misdeeds of the body, you will live." Romans 8:1 says, "Therefore, there is now no condemnation for those who are in Christ Jesus." This gives all Christians reassurance that we are not condemned thanks to Jesus sacrificing His life for us. Although we are all sinners and we all deserve to go to hell, we don't have to. We can choose to follow God and spend eternity in Heaven with Him.

John 3:16-17 says, "For God so loved the world that he gave his one and only Son, that whoever believes in him shall not perish but have eternal life. For God did not send his Son into the world to condemn the world, but to save the world through him." Praise God that we are not condemned!

I have heard people justify their sins by saying that the church is full of Christians who go to church on Sunday morning and then live how they choose to live throughout the week. We must ask ourselves if we truly died to self and have Jesus living through us. If the world cannot see Jesus in us, then we have a problem. If you are trapped in sin and have an attitude that God is a loving God and will forgive and you continue in your sin, there is a problem. Yes, God is a loving and forgiving God but He is also a jealous God and His wrath will come down on those who turn against Him. Do you really want to play Russian roulette with God, the Creator of all, who knows your heart better than you do?

Hebrews 4:12-13 says, "For the word of God is living and active. Sharper than any double-edged sword, it penetrates even to dividing soul and spirit, joints and marrow; it judges the thoughts and attitudes of the heart. Nothing in all creation is hidden from God's sight. Everything is uncovered and laid bare before the eyes of him to whom we must give account." Psalm 44:20-21 tells us, "If we had forgotten the name of our God or spread out our hands to a foreign god, would not God have discovered it, since he knows the secrets of the heart?"

I know of many people who were previously very active in church but they were hurt by another church member or something happened that they disagreed with and they no longer attend church. Non-believers look at this and say that Christians cannot even get along with each other so why should they go to church. Everyone uses excuses. The truth is that we are all human. We all sin and we all make mistakes on a daily basis.

As my pastor says, none of us are good. (He asked someone at church how they were and they responded "good" and he immediately responded that none of us are good, no not one.) Psalm 14:1-3 tells us "The fool says in his heart, 'There is no God.' They are corrupt, their deeds are vile; there is no one who does good. The Lord looks down from heaven on the sons of men to see if there are any who understand, any who seek God. All have turned aside, they have together become corrupt; there is no one who does good, not even one."

We even sometimes put preachers, deacons, teachers "on a pedestal" so to speak. We think that they are perfect and we should follow them. While leaders will be held more accountable, they are not perfect. James 3:1 tells us, "Not many of you should presume to be teachers, my brothers, because you know that we who teach will be judged more strictly." Our pastors are called to be our shepherds; however, pastors are human. Ezekiel 34 explains what happens when the shepherds do not take care of their flocks. We are not to worship any human. We are to worship God and Him alone. We must ensure that we have a personal relationship with God and are not dependent upon our pastor or teacher to fill us with His word. We have to seek His Word on our own.

We do have troubles in churches. We do not always get along with one another. We must be certain that we are not the problem. Are we the one wearing our feelings on our shoulders? Do we get offended at the least little thing that is said to us? Do we then turn and tell others to try to get them on our side? 1 Corinthians 3:3-4 tells us, "You are still worldly. For since there is jealousy and quarreling among you, are you not worldly? Are you not acting like mere men? For when one says, 'I follow Paul,' and another, 'I follow Apollos,' are you not mere men?"

James 5:9 says, "Don't grumble against each other, brothers, or you will be judged. The Judge is standing at the door!" Are we "stirring up dissension" in the church? Proverbs 10:11-13 says, "The mouth of the righteous is a fountain of life, but violence overwhelms the mouth of the wicked. Hatred stirs up dissension, but love covers over all wrongs. Wisdom is found on the lips of the discerning, but a rod is for the back of him who lacks judgment."

We are all human and we all have various opinions but we are still commanded to love one another. Romans 16:17-18 tells us, "I urge you, brothers, to watch out for those who cause divisions and put obstacles in your way that are contrary to the teaching you have learned. Keep away from them. For such people are not serving our Lord Christ, but their own appetites. By smooth talk and flattery they deceive the minds of naive people." Are you the one causing division or putting an obstacle in someone's way?

Think about it. No one thinks that they are the problem. It is always the other person's fault. Well, who exactly is the other person? It's me and you. Are we the problem or the solution? We must be certain without a shadow of a doubt that we are walking with God. We must bring everything to Him in prayer, fervent prayer. 1 Thessalonians 5:16-18 says, "Be joyful always; pray continually; give thanks in all circumstances, for this is God's will for you in Christ Jesus." We must be open and ready to listen to God when He reveals to us that we are the problem. And we must repent and make things right. 2 Timothy 2:16 tells us, "Avoid godless chatter, because those who indulge in it will become more and more ungodly."

Are you in the middle of an argument and your pride will not allow you to concede? We are commanded to be kind to everyone. 2 Timothy 2:23-26 tells us, "Don't have anything to do with foolish and stupid arguments, because you know they produce quarrels. And the Lord's servant must not quarrel; instead, he must be kind to everyone, able to teach, not resentful. Those who oppose him he must gently instruct, in the hope that God will grant them repentance leading them to a knowledge of the truth, and that they will come to their senses and escape from the trap of the devil, who has taken them captive to do his will."

If 10% of our church body is doing 100% of the work, what is the other 90% doing? Are they sitting back waiting to be served? Each member of the body has a special function and each of us needs to be doing his part. We wonder why that 10% of the people doing the work gets burned out. If everyone does his/her part, then the church body will function as instructed in the Bible. Are you one of those sitting around the table waiting to be fed or are you out in the fields doing the work?

If something is not going the way we think it should in the church, we automatically say that the pastor needs to address the problem. Or, we ask, why don't the deacons fix the problem? Then we start murmuring about it and causing dissension. This is one of the ways that Satan is attacking churches. (Yes, I have been there, done that, got the t-shirt, and don't ever want to go back.) I think that everyone who has been involved in a church can identify with this. What if God is calling you to do something about the problem? What if God reveals that you are the problem? Will you allow pride to stand in the way? Do you really want to be Satan's pawn? We must take it to His Throne and allow Him to lead us in His ways. His ways are always best. 2 Corinthians 10:5-6 says, "We demolish arguments and every pretension that sets itself up against the knowledge of God, and we take captive every thought to make it obedient to Christ. And we will be ready to punish every act of disobedience, once your obedience is complete."

We have so many empty, dead churches today. Where have the people gone? Do they get mad about something and leave? I know that God sometimes leads people to other churches. But we must be sure that we are listening to God and not relying on our own feelings. Some people simply say that they are not getting anything out of the sermons or the church. We must ask ourselves what we are putting into it. Are we going to church on Sunday morning out of a feeling of necessity or do we go with a humble heart prepared to worship and to be filled with the Spirit? Are we going to church and asking God with an open heart and mind to speak to us? Or, do we sit in the pew looking at our watch and thinking about what we are going to do for the afternoon? We get out of it what we put into it. Do you forget about God as you leave church or do you focus on Him throughout the day each and every day? Who is first in your life?

Are you involved in a small group Bible Study? If not, get involved. We need close knit Christian friends to study the Bible with and share our hearts with. Often men are not willing to do this because they feel sharing is not "manly". How are you going to be the Godly, Christian, Spiritual leader of the house that you are called to be if you keep everything bottled up inside? We all need to share but I feel that most men struggle with this more than women. It appears easier for women to share with other women. Most men want to keep this façade that they are doing fine and their family is fine while their family is crumbling around them. It is imperative that Christian men step up and start attending small group Bible studies with other men and sharing their hearts.

Many have asked me if God is in control, why did He allow this to happen to me? Like the mother who just lost her child or the child who was molested by his/her own father or the 9 11 tragedy. I cannot explain why things happen but I can assure you that God's grace is always sufficient. 2 Corinthians 12:8-10 says, "Three times I pleaded with the Lord to take it away from me. But he said to me, 'My grace is sufficient for you, for my power is made perfect in weakness.' Therefore I will boast all the more gladly about my weaknesses, so that Christ's power may rest on me. That is why, for Christ's sake, I delight in weaknesses, in insults, in hardships, in persecutions, in difficulties. For when I am weak, then I am strong."

We live in a dark world where Satan has blinded many to the truth. 2 Corinthians 4:4 says, "The god of this age has blinded the minds of unbelievers, so that they cannot see the light of the gospel of the glory of Christ, who is the image of God." James 4:4 says, "You adulterous people, don't you know that friendship with the world is hatred toward God? Anyone who chooses to be a friend of the world becomes an enemy of God." But, Christians can shine in this world because God has already defeated Satan and we can have total faith in Him and Him alone. He will carry us through and He does have a good and perfect plan for our lives if we will just submit to Him. Jeremiah 29:11 tells us, "'For I know the plans I have for you,' declares the LORD, 'plans to prosper you and not to harm you, plans to give you hope and a future.'"

Proverbs 14:12 says, "There is a way that seems right to a man, but in the end it leads to death." We need to be certain that we are following God and not just following the way that seems right to us. God has given us freedom to choose. We can choose to serve and please others or we can choose to serve and please our Heavenly Father. Who will you choose?

I pray that you don't just read this book and throw it aside. I pray that God will use this book to transform you into His image. He has so many blessings for us and He is just waiting for us to come to Him. Will you throw out your idols and give God the place that He deserves in your life? If He can use me, believe me, He can use anyone.

Chapter 3:

Why do we run?

I have not always listened to God the first, second, third, fourth, fifth…time (You get the picture). Looking back, I can see that it would have been so much smoother had I listened but God never gave up on me. God is using each and every one of those trials in my life to teach me and mold me into His image. Genesis 1:27 says, "So God created man in his own image, in the image of God he created him; male and female he created them." As I reflect on my life, I may have known what God was telling me to do but I chose to try it my way first.

I was not always intentionally disobedient to Him. I just wanted many confirmations to make sure it was what God wanted because maybe it was not what I wanted. My Ladies Sunday School class always jokingly says that we need a flashing billboard from God to tell us what direction to turn. The truth is that we have God's Instruction Book, The Bible, to guide us. We really do not need a billboard.

As I write this, I will be honest, I have been thinking about moving. Not only have I thought about moving, I have been looking for other jobs so I could move. It would be so much easier. Of course, I will only go if I feel God leading me. (Ok, I will admit, I have even prayed for God to use me somewhere else and open that door for me to go.) But the truth is that I would be running from my circumstances. As Christians, we are called to take a stand, not to run. 1 Corinthians 15:58 tells us, "Therefore, my dear brothers, stand firm. Let nothing move you. Always give yourselves fully to the work of the Lord, because you know that your labor in the Lord is not in vain."

I even ran for several months from writing this book. I felt God leading me to write this but I came up with many excuses as to why I should not write this book. I finally conceded my excuses and this has been the greatest experience. God has taught me so much even though this book has been written in only 9 days. At one point, I began feeling overwhelmed with writing this and God told me to slow down and enjoy His fellowship. I realize that I may offend some people by this book and I may even alienate myself from my family and friends. But I am tired of running from God. I truly feel that He has called me to write this and He has placed this on my heart. As Christians, this world is not our home.

We often run because of fear or we do not want to face up to our problems. Remember, we are to fear only God, not man. Isaiah 41:10 says, "So do not fear, for I am with you; do not be dismayed, for I am your God. I will strengthen you and help you; I will uphold you with my righteous right hand." Romans 8:31 says, "What, then, shall we say in response to this? If God is for us, who can be against us?" Ephesians 6:11 says, "Put on the full armor of God so that you can take your stand against the devil's schemes."

Sometimes we run because of our own insecurities. I felt God leading me to teach a Ladies Sunday School class approximately 7 years ago; however, I questioned Him and ran. Although I had previously taught youth and I had a degree in education and a Master's degree, I did not feel qualified to teach adults. I also really did not feel secure speaking to a group of adults. As a child, I had a speech impediment and was made fun of tremendously. (My maiden name was Wendy Williams and my brother's name was Ricky. I pronounced our names as "inny ium" and "icky ium." Yes, adults thought this was "cute", so they often had me talk in front of them while they laughed! This was not just something cute that I "outgrew." I had to leave class from first through third grades to attend Speech Therapy. Let me just say that kids can be cruel!) This caused me to feel insecure to speak in public. This was just another of my excuses. God can do anything through us. After several years of trying to "reason" with God, I finally submitted and began teaching the ladies' class.

Currently there is hype about self-confidence and people want to blame their problems on a lack of self-confidence. We should not have confidence in ourselves. We are nothing without God but with Him, we are mighty! 2 Corinthians 3:5 says, "Not that we are competent in ourselves to claim anything for ourselves, but our competence comes from God." Our true source of confidence is from God and we can do anything that He leads us to do with Him. He will always supply us with His strength as long as we are following Him.

I have had many Sundays where I taught through the flesh. Although I had studied my lesson, I did not sincerely seek God to fill me and teach through me. I failed terribly on those Sundays. I simply cannot do it without God. I have learned that I must be totally empty of myself and allow Him to fill me prior to teaching. I did not need a degree to teach His Word. I only need His presence.

I was at a job several years ago and I just really felt lead to do something else. I had been doing the same thing for many years and a position at my employment opened up that I wanted. I began that job and I began having struggles. I was having health problems and my church was having struggles. Of course, my home life was miserable. I had a problematic friendship that caused me great grief. Our dog was run over and killed. (On a side note, health problems are often brought on by stress.) It was honestly a "bad year." I began to seek God more and more. It's truly shameful that sometimes it takes rough times for Him to get our attention. Looking back, I believe God was probably trying to get me to leave that employment then but I chose to do things my way. Once again, I ran.

I hate to admit this, but I had gone through periods in my life where I would get up every morning and study the Bible and pray and go to church every Sunday but I really was not allowing God in my life. This was all like a ritual. It was like checking off things on my to-do list. I was not expecting God to speak to me and I certainly was not ever still for Him to speak to me. I prayed for Him to use me but how could He use me when I was too busy with life to listen to Him? I was a Christian but I had allowed Satan to have a stronghold over me and I was living life for me. That is what society pushes down our throats… "me, me, me…if you're not happy, get out." That is such a lie from the father of lies. We are not here to be happy nor are we here to serve ourselves!

So, at this time in my life when everything seemed to be falling apart, I finally began seeking to get right with God. (I only thought it was falling apart then!) I changed jobs again, all at the same place of employment, of course. After all, I was set in my ways and I could never leave that stable employment with a great paycheck and great benefits. Most people did not ever leave from working there unless they retired or transferred within the system and I originally planned to retire from there.

I was attending a Bible Study during this time and I remember us having a discussion about being a "living sacrifice". Although I was seeking God's will for my life at that time, I was not ready to let go of every area and truly be a "living sacrifice." I even voiced that in the Bible Study that I was not a "living sacrifice." God immediately convicted me of this and I can truly say that I began praying to be a "living sacrifice" shortly after that conviction. Now, think about this. A "living sacrifice" means giving up your life for Him. He gave His life for me so why shouldn't I give my life for Him. It is really not "my life" anyway because I died to myself and He is living through me. That is what Christians are called to do. This is a process that does not happen overnight, especially if you are strong-willed like me. He will reveal to you the areas that you are holding on to. He wants all of you.

As God began to do an amazing work in my life, I became more and more convicted that He wanted me to leave my place of employment. (I must admit that He had to make me absolutely miserable before I conceded my will. I thought I was going to retire there.) I immediately assumed that He wanted to re-locate me and I could just transfer because He certainly was not calling me to leave that job stability. I had worked so hard to receive my Master's Degree and I had been working there for almost 11 years. (Again, I managed to turn it back around to "me, me, me". I know...I'm a slow learner!)

He finally was able to get my attention and He moved me to a job out of the social work field entirely away from my background. Most of my family, friends, and co-workers asked if I had lost my mind. It was inconceivable to them to leave my career with the monetary benefits. I know without a doubt that God called me to this job. That does not mean that many days I have not felt like a square peg trying to fit in a round hole. I have no idea what plans He has for my future but I know that He has a good and perfect plan and if I continue to submit to Him, He will use me wherever He chooses.

We do not always understand the reasons that God calls us to move and we may never know until we get to Heaven. It is ok. We do not need to know everything. We only need to know that God has a good and perfect plan for our lives. Oh, if we could only be at the point and stay at the point of letting God have total control of every area of our lives. We honestly do not have to fret over anything. He takes care of it all. Philippians 4:13 tells us, "I can do everything through him who gives me strength." Even in the midst of my pending divorce, I can look back and see how God has prepared me for this very moment. He has always been with me through each and every trial and He is using every single trial to prepare me for the future. I am in absolute awe of Him.

Sometimes we become complacent in our lives and we do not submit to God. We are scared to "get out of the boat" and surrender to God because we lack faith. We are scared of the "unknown" so we just stay in our "comfort zone." As Christians, we are called to totally surrender to God and have faith that He will guide us through it all. No matter what our circumstances are, God will carry us.

Are you tired of living a humdrum life? Do you feel that you do the same old thing day in and day out and are just spinning your wheels? Give your whole self to God. Give Him every area of your life and you will never be the same. You will not want to ever turn back if you will give Him your all and stay totally focused on Him. Just remember, Satan will still attack but through Jesus, Christians have the power over Satan. James 4:7 tells us, "Submit yourselves, then, to God. Resist the devil, and he will flee from you."

When you are going through a marital crisis, your emotions change before you can blink an eye…and then they change back! This gives a whole new meaning to "emotional rollercoaster." I mean, one second you hate your spouse and the next second you love them. If you've ever been through this, you know exactly what I am talking about. Everything is based on your spouse's response or reaction. If they don't respond like you expect, then the emotions go crazy.

Just imagine for a moment if we gave our emotions totally to God. What if we did not have any expectations of our spouse? What if we place our total and complete trust in God and God alone? God will never let us down. He will never disappoint us. He will never leave us nor forsake us. 2 Thessalonians 3:3 tells us, "But the Lord is faithful, and he will strengthen and protect you from the evil one." Philippians 4:19 says, "And my God will meet all your needs according to his glorious riches in Christ Jesus."

Look at the current divorce rate. Think about how many of your friends and family members are currently going through a divorce. Everyone wants to quit. Everyone wants the easy way out. It's all about "me, me, me." (OK, I realize that I sound hypocritical since I have filed for divorce but I have totally surrendered my marriage to God and my prayer is that God will reconcile my marriage.) Just look at what we have allowed to happen. Christians have sat back and allowed society to dictate our lives. We did not take a stand for marriage because it may step on someone's toes. Well, look at where it got us. We have just as many if not more divorces in our churches as nonbelievers. We are so caught up in our own busyness and "keeping up with the Jones'" that we do not care about our hurting family, friends or neighbors. Everyone is out for "number 1". What a sad world.

Divorce affects our children and history shows us that divorce is cyclical. Children need their father and mother to raise them together. What are we teaching our children about marriage and commitment with our current divorce rate? Children are our heritage and a blessing from God. Psalm 127:3 says, "Sons are a heritage from the Lord, children a reward from him." Since children are a blessing and heritage, why are so many parents more concerned about themselves? We have so many parents who would prefer to be a friend to their child than to be a parent. Ephesians 6:4 says, "Fathers, do not exasperate your children; instead, bring them up in the training and instruction of the Lord."

Kids are a blessing from God. Why are parents today more focused on their own pleasures than being a parent to their children? Why do parents just want to be friends with their children? Look around us at what this has created. Our babies are having babies. Our babies are addicted to drugs and alcohol when they are in Junior High School. Where are our morals? We turn the other cheek and say "that's just what kids do these days". No, that is not acceptable. Proverbs 22:6 tells us, "Train a child in the way he should go, and when he is old he will not turn from it."

I have many friends who are in stale marriages who see their anniversaries come and go without even saying a word to their mate. They are living in absolute misery. Marriage is not supposed to be miserable. Yes, there are trials in marriage because we are all different but we are to work through those trials. Being different is not a reason to get a divorce. It is an excuse. If we all loved our mates as 1 Corinthians 13 says, this would transform our marriages.

Divorce is not the immediate answer. It just appears to be the easy way out. 1 Corinthians 7:10-16 says, "To the married I give this command (not I, but the Lord): A wife must not separate from her husband. But if she does, she must remain unmarried or else be reconciled to her husband. And a husband must not divorce his wife. To the rest I say this (I, not the Lord): If any brother has a wife who is not a believer and she is willing to live with him, he must not divorce her. And if a woman has a husband who is not a believer and he is willing to live with her, she must not divorce him. For the unbelieving husband has been sanctified through his wife, and the unbelieving wife has been sanctified through her believing husband. Otherwise your children would be unclean, but as it is, they are holy. But if the unbeliever leaves, let him do so. A believing man or woman is not bound in such circumstances; God has called us to live in peace. How do you know, wife, whether you will save your husband? Or, how do you know, husband, whether you will save your wife?"

Although I am in the midst of a pending divorce, I do not condone divorce. I do not want a divorce. I am confused as to why God is allowing this to happen since He hates divorce. But I know without a shadow of a doubt that God has a reason for this and He has a good and perfect plan for my life. I do not need to know God's reason and I do not need to know God's plan for my future. I have totally surrendered my marriage to Him and I cannot take it back and try to fix it again. I have caused so much extra heartache for me and my family by doing this. I am joyous and thankful in knowing that God is in control of my future and I am not in control. That means that I can totally let go and not try to control anything. Although I still have tears, I have a peace that is indescribable.

Now, I am not condoning adultery or abuse. If you are being physically abused, you should seek shelter immediately and seek counseling. Mental and emotional abuse can be as bad as physical abuse. God can heal you and your spouse if you will both surrender your marriage to Him. I cannot guarantee that your marriage will be redeemed because only God knows the heart. Only God knows who will sincerely surrender to His will. But if both you and your spouse sincerely surrender to God, I can assure you that your marriage will be wonderful. Yes, you will still have disagreements but with God at the center of your marriage and your life, you will have the marriage that people dream of.

If you are in the midst of marital strife, pray for Godly wisdom in handling your situation. Pray for your spouse and your marriage. Let God have complete control of you, your spouse and your marriage. Allow God to lead each and every decision that you make.

As I attended a seminar for group leaders many years ago, we were told that you only get out of group what you put into group. Well, at the time, I didn't like speaking in a crowd so I was offended by this statement because I had no intention of putting anything into the group. There is a lot of truth to this statement in all areas of life. Do we just sit back and expect to receive everything? We honestly do get out of things what we put in them. If we put nothing into our marriage, we will get nothing out of the marriage. If we are totally self-centered and self-absorbed, how do we expect to show selfless love to our mate? What if your mate thought the thoughts about you that you think about them? What if your mate treated you exactly as you treat them? If you commit adultery, then they commit adultery. Romans 12:19 says, "Do not take revenge, my friends, but leave room for God's wrath, for it is written: 'It is mine to avenge; I will repay,' says the Lord."

Some people appear to have a perfect marriage. There is no such thing. Only Jesus lived on this earth as a perfect human. We cannot possibly agree all of the time about everything. We would be a clone if we did. We can give it to God and allow God to be the center of our marriage and He will salvage our dying marriages. These people who appear to have a perfect marriage, you know them too. It is a façade. We have no clue what goes on behind closed doors because we don't share with each other. We think we are supposed to cover it all up and put on a happy face. This is literally killing us! We cannot continue to suppress everything and put on a show for everyone.

Many years ago, Dennis and I would fellowship with other Christian couples every weekend. We enjoyed being with friends. However, as the years passed, we quit this fellowship. We actually quit doing anything together. We became busy with our children and with life. This was actually an excuse. Dennis told me several weeks ago that he quit doing anything with me because he did not like me. My own husband could not stand to be around me. Over 10 years went by with Dennis having built up resentment and hatred towards me and he never said a word to me about this. Has this happened to your marriage? How do you feel about your spouse right now? Please do not allow one more moment to go by without truly communicating your feelings with your spouse.

I have a friend who thought that she had a perfect marriage; however, she found out that her husband was severely addicted to pornography. Pornography is a huge problem in this day and age especially with the easy access of computers. I have known respectable men in churches who have tried to talk their wives into having a ménage à trois and using pornography with them. This is sin. This is not what God intended in marriages. We have become so worldly that we have accepted this and we must take a stand against it. Sometimes wives are naïve and do not want to upset their husbands so they go along with this. Again, this is sin and not Biblical. Although the man is the head of the household, wives do not have to follow them blindly into sin.

Chapter 4:

When the truth hurts!

❧

Jonah ran from God because he did not want to tell Nineveh the truth. The truth sometimes hurts. I was recently convicted over my situation with Dennis. I was going along with him to not bring up the negative but sometimes we are called to speak the truth even though it hurts. God revealed to me that I was causing my own pain by allowing this control over me. As a Christian, I am to take a stand for the truth. I was actually doing more harm to myself and our relationship by keeping my true feelings bottled up.

Granted, every few days I would explode and tell Dennis about my true feelings and then I would go right back to bottling them up. (I know this is the worst thing to do. As a counselor, I'm probably not the best at taking my own advice!) Since God is the Father of Truth and He cannot tell a lie, how can we as Christians live a lie?

Now, this is not giving everyone the right to go around speaking their mind to everyone they encounter. We have to pray continually and seek God's guidance and wisdom. We must allow God to lead us to speak the truth. We have to be careful that Satan does not have us deceived. Satan is very crafty and he deceives us into believing his lies as the truth. This is the reason that we must pray for God to captivate every thought to make our thoughts holy and pleasing to Him. We must stay in His Word and with Christian friends or Satan will creep right in without our knowledge.

I hate to admit this but even as a Christian it is difficult to identify Satan's lies. I have struggles wanting confirmation that God is speaking to me and not Satan. I know that sounds shameful because I should automatically know my Father's voice but Satan is very deceitful. We must be careful to whose voice we are listening. Matthew 16:23-28 tells us that Jesus referred to Peter as a stumbling block. I feel that Peter probably thought he was doing what was right. We must be very careful that we are not a stumbling block for anyone. We also must be very careful that we do not want something so desperately that we believe that God is telling us to do it. We must pray fervently and stay in His Word and surround ourselves with God-fearing, Christian friends. And, of course, we must be patient and wait for God.

There's that "p" word. My Sunday School class always jokes about not praying for patience. I actually avoided praying for patience for many years because I really did not want God to give me patience. (I knew I would have to persevere through trials to receive patience. Let's face it, I did not want to sacrifice just to gain patience.) Well, God convicted me to pray for patience just a few weeks prior to Dennis telling me about the adultery. My Sunday School class tried to talk me out of it but I knew that God was convicting me and I had to be submissive to Him.

We must be very careful that we are following God and not Satan. When you feel called to speak the truth, make sure you have confirmation from God. Matthew 12:34-37 says, "You brood of vipers, how can you who are evil say anything good? For out of the overflow of the heart the mouth speaks. The good man brings good things out of the good stored up in him, and the evil man brings evil things out of the evil stored up in him. But I tell you that men will have to give account on the day of judgment for every careless word they have spoken. For by your words you will be acquitted, and by your words you will be condemned." We will be held accountable for every careless word we have spoken. This should make us stop and think about what we say prior to speaking.

If you think that you are being a "true friend" or that someone else is your "true friend" because they listen to you and appear to agree with you even in the midst of your sin, this is not true friendship. True friends will tell you when you are wrong and gently guide you back to God. If you are a "feel good friend" who does not have the nerve to speak the truth for fear of losing the friend, seek God's guidance. If you fear you will lose a friendship over speaking the truth, what kind of friendship do you truly have? The truth does sometimes hurt. Some friends do not want to hear the truth but we are not being a friend if we do not speak the truth.

We can be so deceived that we actually believe a lie as the truth. Have you ever told a lie? We sometimes justify "a little white lie" because we do not want to hurt someone's feelings. Even a "little white lie" is wrong. These turn into "bigger" lies. (Who do we think we are to rank a lie or a sin? I mean, a lie is a lie and a sin is a sin and a lie is sin. We all have lied and we all have sinned.) Sometimes we tell a lie and then it snowballs. We get trapped and then tell another lie and another lie. Then we do not see a way out. We feel that we have to keep up the lies for fear of the truth being known. This is how Satan deceives us.

As if telling the lies is not bad enough, then we turn it around and blame others. We become angry with the person that we lied to because they asked too many questions or because we know that they have caught us and our pride will not allow us to tell the truth. This is all from Satan. God is the Father of Truth. Satan is the father of lies. Who will you choose to follow? Telling a lie is a sin. There are no excuses. What if every Christian chose right now to never tell a lie? With God's strength, we can stop telling lies. If we sincerely ask God to help us to always tell the truth, the Holy Spirit will convict us when we lie and eventually, we will stop telling lies.

A few months ago, I was checking up on Dennis since there was no trust there. I called his work and asked for him because I did not believe that he was there. (Yes, I was sneaky and used the *67 so my number would not show up on the caller ID.) Well, he was there and I immediately hung up the phone when the employee went to get him. When Dennis arrived home, he asked me if I had called his work. I do not know why I did this but I responded "no." For some reason, I did not want him to know that I had checked up on him. Oh, I cannot describe the guilt that I was overwhelmed with. I felt terrible. Within the hour, I had totally confessed to him. I was literally eaten alive with guilt. Dennis actually laughed at me.

Now, that may seem like an innocent lie when you look at adultery and all of the other lies that have been involved in our marriage. But no lie is innocent. A lie is a lie. Once we tell a lie and then another, we eventually quit listening when the Holy Spirit convicts us and telling a lie becomes a habit. Just because Dennis has told many lies does not make it right for me to lie to him.

Could we possibly be so buried in our own problems and grief that we cannot even see the truth when it is right in front of us? Jesus' own disciples were so grief stricken after His death that they did not even recognize Him when he was in their presence and walking and talking with them. Can we be that blind?

My entire life I have had a pet peeve about lying. I could not stand to be lied to and I felt that it was my duty to confront the person and get the truth out. God has taught me so much. It is not "my duty" to always reveal the truth.

I must leave that up to God and if He leads me to confront someone about telling a lie, then I can do it in His power. It appears ironic that I have always hated lies and now I am living with a husband who chooses to lie to me. But, we know that nothing is ironic. God causes everything to happen for a reason. Romans 8:28 says, "And we know that in all things God works for the good of those who love him, who have been called according to his purpose."

If Jesus is truly living in you, the Holy Spirit will convict you when you tell a lie and give you a repentant heart. Remember, repentance means to turn from the sin. That means you stop. You will not be able to continue telling lies. We sometimes excuse telling a lie and just say that it is a habit. There is no excuse. We must submit this to God. Telling a lie will cause our hearts to harden and blind us to the truth. 1 John 3:7-10 tells us, "Dear children, do not let anyone lead you astray. He who does what is right is righteous, just as he is righteous. He who does what is sinful is of the devil, because the devil has been sinning from the beginning. The reason the Son of God appeared was to destroy the devil's work. No one who is born of God will continue to sin, because God's seed remains in him; he cannot go on sinning, because he has been born of God. This is how we know who the children of God are and who the children of the devil are: Anyone who does not do what is right is not a child of God; nor is anyone who does not love his brother." Are you living like a child of God?

Galatians 5:16-18 says, "So I say, live by the Spirit, and you will not gratify the desires of the sinful nature. For the sinful nature desires what is contrary to the Spirit, and the Spirit what is contrary to the sinful nature. They are in conflict with each other, so that you do not do what you want. But if you are led by the Spirit, you are not under law."

Stop and think what this world would be like, or even what our homes, churches and work places would be like, if every professing Christian never told a lie. This could change the world. In this "sue happy world", imagine what telling the truth would do to all of these lawsuits. James 5:12 says, "Above all, my brothers, do not swear—not by heaven or by earth or by anything else. Let your 'Yes' be yes, and your 'No,' no, or you will be condemned." As Christians, we are instructed to keep our word. We should not tell a lie and we should keep our commitments.

Sometimes, we simply do not want to face the truth. We want everything "sugarcoated". We want this fairytale life. The truth is that my marriage may end in divorce. No, that is not God's perfect will and no, this is not what I want. However, God has given us the freedom of choice and sometimes we do not make the right choices. We may be totally blinded and think that we are following God but remember that Satan is deceptive. This saddens me but I know that God is in control and God will provide. The truth is that we live in a world full of hardened hearts with a "me-first" mentality. Satan is the father of this cruel world but there is no need to despair because God prevails.

Most of my friends and family have thought that I was absolutely crazy for trying to make my marriage work. After all, it had been a miserable marriage for at least 13 of the 17 years. Their view was that maybe this was a Godsend because they knew that I would not divorce because it was not Biblical but now I could justify my divorce since Dennis committed adultery. (I believe that just the act of adultery does not warrant a divorce. If there is a truly repentant heart, there should not be a divorce.) This was my chance to get out of my misery. I was asked by some "are you desperate?" and many advised me to throw out all of Dennis' belongings in the yard and change the locks on the house. I realize the natural "human" response is to get revenge but that is not God's response. 1 Peter 3:9 tells us, "Do not repay evil with evil or insult with insult, but with blessing, because to this you were called so that you may inherit a blessing."

This has caused a huge strain on my relationship with family and some friends. But I have spent so much time with God in seeking His will and not the world's will. Not only is God my Heavenly Father but He is my best friend. I talk to Him throughout each and every day (and often times throughout the night). He is the only One that I needed all along. I do have one Christian friend who also kept encouraging me to "hang in there." Thank you, Andrea, for being a God-fearing woman and a wonderful Christian friend. (God put her in my life when He knew I would need her most. I did not always want to hear what she said but I know it was always Biblical and God was using her.)

Having an affair is not God's will. Divorce is not God's will. He allows these things to happen because He gives us free will. We make the choices. I actually defended Dennis for months after the affair saying that Satan had a stronghold over him and he was blinded to the truth. You know the old saying "the devil made me do it." While that may be true, he made the choice to commit adultery and continue in the affair. He made the choice to lie to me and to repeatedly lie to me. There are no excuses. God always gives us a way out of temptation. 1 Corinthians 10:12-13 tells us, "So, if you think you are standing firm, be careful that you don't fall! No temptation has seized you except what is common to man. And God is faithful; He will not let you be tempted beyond what you can bear. But when you are tempted, he will also provide a way out so that you can stand up under it."

We cannot keep making up excuses as this enables the person to continue in their sin when we do this. We must take responsibility for our own actions. We cannot blame others or God. I have actually caused a lot of my own heart ache because I was trying to fix everything instead of totally surrendering it to God. I made that choice and I have to accept responsibility and live with the consequences.

However, Christians need not despair because Jesus' death on the cross and then His resurrection paid the price for our sins. Not only did He pay the price for our sins but He gave us freedom to live in Him. Christians are on the winning team. Satan has already been defeated. Christians do not have anything to worry about or to fret over. We have the freedom to let go of all of our burdens and give them to God. My nature was to want to know what to expect so I can prepare myself. I have learned to let that go. I do not need to know the future nor do I need to prepare myself for anything. God not only knows the future but He controls the future. I need to have total faith in Him for the future. If I knew the future, that would not take any faith. Hebrews 11:1 tells us, "Now faith is being sure of what we hope for and certain of what we do not see." Romans 10:17 says, "Consequently, faith comes from hearing the message, and the message is heard through the word of Christ." 2 Corinthians 5:7 tells us, "We live by faith, not by sight."

For months, I kept saying that I felt like I was dying inside. I finally realized that I had it all wrong. I was dying on the outside. I was dying to myself. It was a very painful process but words cannot explain how free I feel at this very moment. Although my circumstances have not changed, I feel a peace and love within myself that I cannot even comprehend. Praise the Lord!

Colossians 3:1-10 tells us, "Since, then, you have been raised with Christ, set your hearts on things above, where Christ is seated at the right hand of God. Set your minds on things above, not on earthly things. For you died, and your life is now hidden with Christ in God. When Christ, who is your life, appears, then you also will appear with him in glory. Put to death, therefore, whatever belongs to your earthly nature: sexual immorality, impurity, lust, evil desires and greed, which is idolatry. Because of these, the wrath of God is coming. You used to walk in these ways, in the life you once lived. But now you must rid yourselves of all such things as these: anger, rage, malice, slander, and filthy language from your lips. Do not lie to each other, since you have taken off your old self with its practices and have put on the new self, which is being renewed in knowledge in the image of its Creator." Have you truly died to yourself? Are you allowing Jesus to live through you?

Chapter 5:

Is the fine line invisible?

There is a fine line between forgiveness and forgetting. Let's face it. It is not humanly possible to totally forget but God's grace allows us to forgive. We can forgive someone; however, it does not mean that we condone their behavior. Forgiveness does not mean that we must agree with what they have done. I have totally forgiven Dennis for his affairs and for the continuous lies. This does not mean that I have given him the right to continue in affairs or to continue to lie to me. Forgiveness does not mean that we are a doormat to be taken advantage of and walked all over. As a Christian, forgiveness is not an option, it is a command. We are to continually forgive every time someone wrongs us. However, as I said, forgiving someone does not give them the approval to continue in their actions.

There is a fine line between grace and pseudo grace. Christians often think of grace as overlooking the sin and loving anyway. However, if the person does not have a truly repentant heart (this is only for God to judge), we often enable that person to continue in their sin by overlooking the sin and not helping the person deal with the sin properly. Only God can give a repentant heart and only God can remove sin. We may try to do these things on our own but again, we mess up. We can repeatedly try to do outwardly things to make up for our sin but if it is not coming from the heart, it is meaningless. Remember, God knows our hearts. We cannot hide anything from Him.

There is a fine line between extending mercy and being "played a fool". I grew up being told to never call anyone a fool. I am not referring to anyone as a fool but we do have to look at how frequently the word "fool" is used in the Bible. Do you really think that anyone sets their goal in life to be a "fool"? No, these people are deceived by Satan and they often have no clue that they are following Satan. Remember that Satan is the father of this world and he is deceitful. Proverbs 1:31-33 tells us, "they will eat the fruit of their ways and be filled with the fruit of their schemes. For the waywardness of the simple will kill them, and the complacency of fools will destroy them; but whoever listens to me will live in safety and be at ease, without fear of harm." It is easy for us to point fingers at the "fools" in our lives but we need to ask God to reveal to us if we are the "fool."

A few months ago, I was reading 2 books at the same time. I was just desperately seeking answers. I had one book that basically said to forgive and forget. The other book was about setting boundaries and taking a stand to the "fools" in our lives. I was so confused after reading those 2 books. They were both excellent, Christian books with great points but they were on the opposite ends of the spectrum. I thought that surely there is a "happy medium" and I wondered how many people just read one of those books and then make a major life decision based on that one book. We must seek our answers from God and Him alone. God provides us all of the answers that we need in His Word. Although we do not always receive immediate answers, we are assured that if we fervently seek Him, He will answer us.

There is a fine line between the sheep and the wolves in sheep clothing. Only God knows the heart. We are not here to judge but God knows and God will reveal the truth. Titus 1:15-16 says, "To the pure, all things are pure, but to those who are corrupted and do not believe, nothing is pure. In fact, both their minds and consciences are corrupted. They claim to know God, but by their actions they deny him. They are detestable, disobedient and unfit for doing anything good." Are you pure or corrupted?

There is a fine line between speaking the truth and being perceived as "judgmental". After Dennis told me about the affair, I felt led numerous times to call him and share scripture with him. I just could not fathom how a Christian could be so deceived by Satan. How could a Christian believe that he could pray for forgiveness prior to committing adultery and then say that they know they are forgiven? I was accused of being judgmental so I bit my tongue. Many times, I did not take a stand for God's Word even when I felt led because I did not want to be perceived as being judgmental. We are to gently speak the truth and not fear what man thinks of us. However, we do need to be led by God and not go around condemning everyone. Actually we cannot condemn anyone because we are not God but we can allow Him to speak the truth through us.

I was living in fear of displeasing Dennis instead of fear of displeasing God. I turned it all around in my mind and justified my actions by saying that God hates divorce and I needed to save my marriage. Yes, God does hate divorce but I can't save my marriage. Only God can. I must totally surrender my marriage to God. I also thought that I could "sacrifice" myself and my feelings. I thought this would be such a testimony…"Look what I did." Yes, please look at what I did…I made an even bigger mess. I have enabled sin to continue by allowing myself to be a "door mat." I can blame no one but myself because I made these choices. Again, these were my actions and not God's plan.

There is nothing that I can do to salvage this dead marriage. But I have total and complete faith that God can redeem my marriage and make it absolutely beautiful and wonderful. Yes, I am talking about my marriage to Dennis! God wants the full glory for what He will do. I will not nor do I need any glory for anything. I have done nothing but make a mess in my own strength.

Looking back, I should have listened to God and dealt with all of this God's way. I was trying desperately to make my husband think that I was not a "holy roller". I would even sit and watch television with him instead of reading my Bible which is what I felt led to do because I did not want Dennis to think I was some "religious freak." The truth is that I am a "Jesus freak" if that is what you want to call me. I need to read His Word constantly right now because I need His guidance. However, I have no regrets because God has used every situation to teach me.

We must submit to God to find the answers. I certainly do not have the answers. Only God can provide you with the answer in your specific situation. You see, God knows all and sees all. God may be doing a work in someone's heart next to you and He may use you this very day to speak to that person without you even knowing. God will give you guidance and He will reveal to you where the lines are and where they need to be.

I have to stop for a second in awe of God. I just cannot fathom why anyone would not choose to follow Him. He is the Creator of everything and He created us in His image. Genesis 1:27 tells us, "So God created man in his own image, in the image of God he created him; male and female he created them." He knows the past, present and future. He is in total control. How could anyone be so prideful and arrogant that they would believe that their way is better than

God's way? I know that Satan has some deceived but you can make a choice to break free from Satan and turn to God. God always provides a way out of temptation. It all goes back to the choices that we make.

Chapter 6:

Why can't I change him or her?

‿❧

Toes get prepared to be stepped on! As I mentioned before, I had a list of things that I thought that Dennis should do to try to reconcile our marriage. The things that I wanted him to do were actually to help him and his relationship with God. I told him from the beginning that I was far more concerned about his relationship with God than with me because God is far more important. (Could I have been a little selfish in that because I knew that God hates divorce and the marriage would work out?)

Dennis had a list of things for me to change as well... things that he did not like about me such as my obsessive-compulsive nature. Well, I began letting go of things and trying to change for Dennis. After several months, I finally realized I am never going to please him. I did not need to change for him. I need to allow God to change me into God's image not into the image that Dennis wanted. I have let go of a lot of my obsessive-compulsive tendencies. I know my friends and former co-workers would find that hard to believe but they have not seen my desk at work! God had me change jobs only 3 months before Dennis told me about the adultery.

God planned that for many reasons that I can see and probably many that I cannot yet see. If anyone knows my current boss, they will laugh because it is not possible to be obsessive-compulsive and work with him (and keep your sanity).

Although the things that I wanted Dennis to do would have been good for his Christian walk, I cannot change Dennis. I am not God. Only God can change someone. If Dennis had done the things I requested, would I have wanted the glory? Only God deserves glory. We do not deserve anything. We are blessed that God chooses to use us but God alone deserves the glory. If God reconciles my marriage, it will truly be a miracle and God will receive all of the glory.

Men and women think totally differently. I am not saying that one is way is right or wrong. We are just different. Sometimes this causes friction in our marriages because we just cannot understand why our spouse would do or say the things they do or say. We need to have open communication. We need to be able to freely discuss our true feelings with our spouse. Open communication is vital for a healthy marriage.

Are we telling God that He messed up when we want someone to change and conform to our image? God created everyone. God knows us inside and out. God loves us all the same. We need to pray for God to allow us to love the person that we want to change through God's eyes. Pray to see them through God's eyes. This is not easy but it is necessary for healing.

Why do we get married and think that we can change someone? I hear of people so often saying that their mate will change after their marriage. Wrong! The only way for anyone to change is for God to change them. Now, people may outwardly appear to change for a little while trying to prove a point but only God can change the heart and true change must come from the heart.

How can we be so prideful and arrogant to think that we are right and they are wrong? That is what we are saying when we want them to change. We are saying that our way is better than their way and they need to change over to our way. What makes you think that you are right? Matthew 22:39b tells us to "love your neighbor as yourself."

We must give ourselves totally to God and allow God to change us. I have given God my total being. (That is not to say I do not sometimes take it back but that is addressed in another chapter.) We must be accountable for our own actions and take responsibility. Yes, I could wallow in self-pity for the things that Dennis has done to me. But the fact is that I have made the choice to allow him to do these things to me. So, I cannot blame anyone but myself.

What if what we are seeing in our spouse, friend, family member, or co-worker is actually a misperception? What if we are projecting our own thoughts or attitudes onto them? Remember that when we point a finger at someone we always have 3 fingers pointing back at ourselves. What if we are the problem? What if every professing Christian actually allowed God to have complete control of their lives? What if we allowed God to tear down the walls in our hearts and let His love, peace, mercy, joy and patience fill us and live through us? Would the world be a different place? Would non-believers want to be like believers?

Blaming has been around from the beginning. Remember the Garden of Eden? When God asked Adam about eating from the tree, Adam blamed Eve and Eve blamed the serpent. Then we blame Adam and Eve for being banned from the Garden of Eden. Let us quit blaming others and take responsibility for our own actions. We make the choices to do what we do. Christians can give all of our choices to God and we will be assured to follow His good and perfect will.

Some people are master manipulators. They are able to turn any situation around and blame someone else. It does not do any good to argue with these people or even try to understand them. Just think, if you understand them, that would mean that you think like them. We need to pray fervently for these people for God to open their eyes and hearts to the truth.

Luke 6:41-42 tells us, "Why do you look at the speck of sawdust in your brother's eye and pay no attention to the plank in your own eye? How can you say to your brother, 'Brother, let me take the speck out of your eye,' when you yourself fail to see the plank in your own eye? You hypocrite, first take the plank out of your eye, and then you will see clearly to remove the speck from your brother's eye." Have you removed the plank from your own eye?

We are all made in God's image. He created each one of us as a special and unique individual. We are all different. This means that marriage is extremely difficult because we will not always see "eye to eye." We have to learn to "agree to disagree." God loves each and every one of us and He even has the hairs on our heads numbered. (Which would appear to be a difficult task in itself when you think about how much of our hair falls out daily but nothing is difficult for God.)

Matthew 10:30 tells us, "And even the very hairs of your head are all numbered." Psalm 139:2 says, "You know when I sit and when I rise; you perceive my thoughts from afar." (This truly amazes me because I do not understand my own thoughts most of the time.) He loves us no matter our thoughts or actions. He knows all of our idiosyncrasies and loves us anyway. He knows us better than we know ourselves and He wants what is best for us. Since He knows and understands all of our thoughts, why do we try to hide them from Him? Hebrews 4:13 says, "Nothing in all creation is hidden from God's sight. Everything is uncovered and laid bare before the eyes of him to whom we must give account."

There is not a single thought that goes through our minds that God does not know. He knows our hearts, our thoughts, He knows everything. We cannot hide from Him nor should we want to. If we totally submit to Him, we have nothing to fear. At a single word, God can move a mountain. He is the Creator of everything and He knows the past, present and future. We have nothing to lose and everything to gain if we choose Him.

Luke 6:27-31 says, "But I tell you who hear me: Love your enemies, do good to those who hate you, bless those who curse you, pray for those who mistreat you. If someone strikes you on one cheek, turn to him the other also. If someone takes your cloak, do not stop him from taking your tunic. Give to everyone who asks you, and if anyone takes what belongs to you, do not demand it back. Do to others as you would have them do to you." Do you treat everyone as you want to be treated? This includes your spouse, family, friends, co-workers...everyone. Sometimes we treat strangers or acquaintances better than we treat our own family. We are to love everyone and treat everyone as we want to be treated. Why do we treat acquaintances better than our own family?

If we try on our own, we will fail. But God can change us. We need to allow God to not only change us but to totally transform us into His image. What if everyone actually followed the instructions in the Bible? We would see a major transformation in our homes, churches, neighborhoods, and the world.

I have recently learned what it truly means to be burdened over lost souls. Do you have a family member or friend who is lost? Oh what pain and agony it brings to know that someone that we love is going to hell unless they repent and turn to God. We want so desperately to save them but they must make the choice to follow God. We must keep praying for them and allow God to use us as a witness through how we live our lives.

Just saying "this is the way I've always been and I'm not changing" is just an excuse. God does not accept excuses.

Allow God to change you to be the person that He wants you to be. There is no greater joy and peace than to know without a doubt that you are doing exactly what God has called you to do. Do not get frustrated when you fall, let God pick you up and keep going. Notice I said "when" and not "if" because we all fall all the time! We are human. But when we stay down and say "I can't" we are using an excuse. We can't but God can if we let Him.

If each of us actually put others ahead of ourselves, our homes would be a happier place and the world would be better. Philippians 2:3-7 says, "Do nothing out of selfish ambition or vain conceit, but in humility consider others better than yourselves. Each of you should look not only to your own interests, but also to the interests of others. Your attitude should be the same as that of Christ Jesus: Who, being in very nature God, did not consider equality with God something to be grasped, but made himself nothing, taking the very nature of a servant, being made in human likeness." Do you look to your own interests or to the interests of others?

Our homes would change drastically if we all lived by the fruits of the Spirit. Galatians 5:22-23 says, "But the fruit of the Spirit is love, joy, peace, patience, kindness, goodness, faithfulness, gentleness and self-control. Against such things there is no law." 1 Corinthians 10:24 tells us, "Nobody should seek his own good, but the good of others." Titus 3:14 says, "Our people must learn to devote themselves to doing what is good, in order that they may provide for daily necessities and not live unproductive lives." Are you living a productive or unproductive life?

Philippians 2:14 tells us, "Do everything without complaining or arguing." This means that we are not to complain about our housework or errands or argue over anything. Wow. That would be a wonderful home! Husbands and wives should help each other with all of the duties. We need to share all of the responsibilities. It is so overwhelming to work and manage a family. We need to work together and take the load off of our partner. By the way men, it is not called "baby sitting" when you are watching your own children! (Sorry, I had to throw that in there.)

Ok. By now you are asking, what planet did she come from? You are probably even saying that I need to take off my "rose colored glasses" and face reality. Reality is that we need to make some changes in this world and why not start from within? I'm hesitating to share the following because I know women do not like to hear the word submissive but it is Biblical. Ephesians 5:22-29 says, "Wives, submit to your husbands as to the Lord. For the husband is the head of the wife as Christ is the head of the church, his body, of which he is the Savior. Now as the church submits to Christ, so also wives should submit to their husbands in everything. Husbands, love your wives, just as Christ loved the church and gave himself up for her to make her holy, cleansing her by the washing with water through the word, and to present her to himself as a radiant church, without stain or wrinkle or any other blemish, but holy and blameless. In this same way, husbands ought to love their wives as their own bodies. He who loves his wife loves himself. After all, no one ever hated his own body, but he feeds and cares for it, just as Christ does the church."

Let's face it. Most of us do not like change. We are set in our ways and we think that our ways are best. We make up excuses not to change. We even get angry at people who mention change. Change is all around. Look at how much this world has changed just in the last 30 years. Are we still riding in a horse and buggy and using telegrams? Change can be good. I am not that old (in my own eyes) but I learned to type on a manual typewriter where long necklaces would get caught up in the keys. Now we cannot even think about how we made it without computers.

We must get over our self-centered, egotistical attitudes and let God reveal the truth to us. It may be painful in the beginning but the resulting peace and joy is well worth the pain. Make Psalm 139:23-24 your daily heartfelt prayer: "Search me, O God, and know my heart; test me and know my anxious thoughts. See if there is any offensive way in me, and lead me in the way everlasting."

Chapter 7:

Why is it so hard to let go and leave it with God?

❧

I know that I have previously created a mess and then when I could not "fix-it", I would nonchalantly ask God to fix-it for me! I really did not seek God's answer, I just asked for him to fix my mess and I told him how I preferred the outcome. I know this sounds awful but I have done that many, many times throughout my life. And then the nerve of me, I would get mad at God for not fixing my mess the way that I told Him to. Can anyone identify with me here? I was not truly seeking God and His will. I just wanted my situation fixed to my liking.

I have also sincerely been broken and given a problem to God. But when He did not give me the answer that I wanted in my timeframe, I took it back. My control issues and want to "fix it" attitude can really get me in a bind. I also want things in my timeframe. I mean, come on, God's timing takes forever! But His timing is perfect. I cannot fathom that because I am a greedy human. His answers are perfect. What I think would be a good answer to my problem may not be a good answer at all. God sees "the whole picture". He knows the past, present and future and he puts it all together and gives us His best…not just our "good answer" but His good and perfect will.

Could we possibly be so arrogant that we think our way is better than God's way? By taking it back, isn't that what we are saying? We are saying, "Well, God, I gave you a chance and You did not do anything so give it back to me so I can fix it." I know this sounds ridiculous but this is what we do. I kept doing this with my marriage. I would let Dennis go and then he did not appear to turn to God so I would call him back and I would try a little harder. God does not need me. I was not totally giving it to God. I thought that I was doing the right thing and it appeared that I was doing the "Christian thing" but that is not what God wanted. I was not putting my complete faith in God. God alone knows the heart and God alone can change the heart. No one else can do this.

We also say that we have given something to God but we truly have not. We have said a shallow prayer saying that we gave it to Him and then we went on about our business totally ignoring what God wanted us to do. We go on working, running errands, watching television and totally avoiding any quiet time with God. This is not truly giving something to God. We have to get our heart right with Him and submit to His will, not ours. We have to be still and listen to God. Psalm 46:10 says, "Be still, and know that I am God; I will be exalted among the nations, I will be exalted in the earth." How can God guide us if we do not spend any time listening to Him?

We often begin to worry over problems when we feel that God is not answering them in the way that we want. Worrying and stress go hand in hand. Someone once said that worrying is like rocking in a rocking chair, you go back and forth but get nowhere. So, why do we worry? Do we worry because we do not trust God? How can we say that we trust God and still worry?

Philippians 4:6-7 says, "Do not be anxious about anything, but in everything, by prayer and petition, with thanksgiving, present your requests to God. And the peace of God, which transcends all understanding, will guard your hearts and your minds in Christ Jesus." Christians should not be anxious about anything. 1 Peter 5:7 tells us, "Cast all your anxiety on Him because he cares for you." Wow, we can give all of our anxiety to Him because He cares for us.

I have experienced numerous health problems through the years and I now have no doubt that they were due to stress. I have no one to blame but myself. I allowed my stressful marriage and my controlling personality to cause health problems. The whole time I thought that I was giving everything to God and living for God. I was so deceived. God truly wants all of our burdens and anxieties. He does not want us to be anxious about anything. If we totally surrender to Him and we know that He is in control of the future, then what do we have to worry about? Nothing.

Matthew 6:25-34 tells us, "Therefore I tell you, do not worry about your life, what you will eat or drink; or about your body, what you will wear. Is not life more important than food, and the body more important than clothes? Look at the birds of the air; they do not sow or reap or store away in barns, and yet your heavenly Father feeds them. Are you not much more valuable than they? Who of you by worrying can add a single hour to his life? And why do you worry about clothes? See how the lilies of the field grow. They do not labor or spin. Yet I tell you that not even Solomon in all his splendor was dressed like one of these. If that is how God clothes the grass of the field, which is here today and tomorrow is thrown into the fire, will he not much more clothe you, O you of little faith? So do not worry, saying, 'What shall we eat?' or 'What shall we drink?' or 'What shall we wear?' For the pagans run after all these things, and your heavenly Father knows that you need them. But seek first his kingdom and his righteousness, and all these things will be given to you as well. Therefore do not worry about tomorrow, for tomorrow will worry about itself. Each day has enough trouble of its own." Do you find yourself worrying about tomorrow? If God is in control of our lives, we do not need to worry about anything.

Do we really think we know better than God? Would we really tell God, "Oh, I don't think You are handling that correctly, so I will do it my way." We laugh about that but this is what we do every single day when we do not surrender to God and obey Him.

We say we give everything to God but our lives are so full of sin. We live exactly how we choose and we totally ignore God. It's our choice. There are no excuses. We ask for God's blessings but we do not choose to do what His Word tells us to do. We want everything for "me, me, me" but we do not want the consequences of our sins. We must take responsibility for our actions and accept the consequences of our sins. Quit blaming everyone else. Jeremiah 10:23 tells us, "I know, O Lord, that a man's life is not his own; it is not for man to direct his steps." Proverbs 16:9 says, "In his heart, a man plans his course, but the Lord determines his steps."

I went to the Ear, Nose and Throat (ENT) doctor yesterday after not being able to hear out of my ear for several months. I had been treated a month ago for an ear infection by the primary doctor so I just assumed that my infection did not go away. The ENT doctor looked in my ear said "you're not going to like me." He said that he had to clean out my ear and he stuck the vacuum in my ear and cleaned it. (OK, I know it is not called a vacuum but that is what it felt like.) Anyway, I had a huge ball of wax covering my eardrum.

How often do we have something blocking us from hearing from God? Often times, we are so deceived by Satan that we have a "huge ball of wax" (sin) causing us to be hearing impaired to God's voice. We may think that we have an infection (problem in life); however, our problem is actually that our hearing is blocked from God. We may even think that we are listening to God but we cannot hear Him when our communication is blocked.

Is your fellowship cut off from God due to unconfessed sin? 1 Corinthians 3:18 tells us, "Do not deceive yourselves. If any one of you thinks he is wise by the standards of this age, he should become a 'fool' so that he may become wise." Please stop right now and ask God to reveal any barriers to your communication with Him. You can make the choice to get your heart right with God this very moment. It is only too late after you die.

Who are we kidding? God knows our heart, he knows our thoughts before we even think them...we cannot hide from Him. We have no idea what blessings we are missing out on from God because we are selfishly choosing to go our own way. He has blessings just waiting for us if we will only submit to Him and obey Him. This is not our will but His will, His good and perfect will for each of us. We must wait patiently on His timing. We must let Him convict us and draw us to Him. We must pray continually. We cannot base our feelings on the actions of others and we cannot react to situations. We must allow God to guide our actions so we never have to react.

We cannot bargain with God. We cannot comprehend His ways. They are much greater than our ways. I will admit that when I finally accepted that God wanted me to lead that Bible Study, I had in my mind that He was going to fix my marriage if I led that Bible Study. No, He did not tell me that. It was just my carnal mind thinking if I submit to what He is calling me to do, then surely He will give me what I want. Well, the Bible Study was a 13 week course and at the end of the course, my marriage was still in the same situation. God taught me so much through that Bible Study. He knew that I needed that study. I did not need my marriage fixed at that time. I needed to learn more about God and how to be totally dependent on Him and Him alone. (That independency thing has been very hard for me to let go of but I'm still learning and He has not given up on me.) He always knows what is best for us. Remember, He knows the past, present, and future.

2 Chronicles 15:26 says, "The Lord is with you when you are with Him. If you seek Him, He will be found by you, but if you forsake Him, He will forsake you." We must be with Him and seek Him. The only alternative is our unwise choice to forsake Him and I do not even want to think about being forsaken by Him. Galatians 3:3-4 tells us, "Are you so foolish? After beginning with the Spirit, are you now trying to attain your goal by human effort? Have you suffered so much for nothing—if it really was for nothing?" Are you trying to attain your goals by yourself or are you relying on God's guidance?

I was baking a cake this morning for my Sunday School class. I love to bake. As usual, I was trying to multi-task and I did not really focus on the recipe. I mixed the first 2 ingredients together and then I read that one of those ingredients was actually to be stirred in last. (You would think I would have then stopped and read the whole recipe.) I kept going and then realized that I mixed some other ingredients that were supposed to be alternated in the mixing process. I finished the mixing and put it in the oven.

After I cleaned up my mess, I opened my microwave and found the cream cheese that I was softening that belonged in the Cream Cheese Pound Cake that was in the oven. I checked the cake that had been baking for 20 minutes and it was still runny. I dumped it all back in the mixing bowl and added the cream cheese and then put it back in the oven. I had to re-wash the bundt pan and the mixing bowl. The cake ended up turning out ok. (By the way, I was in a hurry and had thought that I would put the cake in the oven and then do my morning Bible study. I usually do my Bible study every morning immediately when I awaken before I start my day.)

Baking this cake is a lot like life. We try to take short cuts and we do not always read the instructions before we dive head first into something. The Bible is our instruction book for life. Although the cake turned out, our lives do not always turn out the way we want. We can cause much pain and grief on ourselves and others because we do not follow His instructions. We often go through our day without focusing on the task at hand. We are too busy thinking about the next task. Are we so busy in this life that we are constantly thinking of "what's next" or daydreaming about what we could be doing? Do we seek God initially or do we only seek God half-heartedly after we have created a mess?

God can and will use every circumstance for His Glory if we just let Him. Why do we search for answers when God has all of the answers waiting for us? He does not want us to settle for second best. Galatians 2:20 tells us, "I have been crucified with Christ and I no longer live, but Christ lives in me. The life I live in the body, I live by faith in the Son of God, who loved me and gave himself for me." Christians have died to sin and we allow God to live through us.

God is our Creator. He created us in His image and He alone is worthy to be praised. Psalm 8:1-9 tells us, "O Lord, our Lord, how majestic is your name in all the earth! You have set your glory above the heavens. From the lips of children and infants you have ordained praise because of your enemies, to silence the foe and the avenger. When I consider your heavens, the work of your fingers, the moon and the stars, which you have set in place, what is man that you are mindful of him, the son of man that you care for him? You made him a little lower than the heavenly beings and crowned him with glory and honor. You made him ruler over the works of your hands; you put everything under his feet: all flocks and herds, and the beasts of the field, the birds of the air, and the fish of the sea, all that swim the paths of the seas. O Lord, our Lord, how majestic is your name in all the earth!"

God uses ordinary lives to do extraordinary things if we allow Him. I feel God leading me to write this book and share my heart. I have experienced numerous doubts as I was writing this that I am not a writer; However, God convicted me that I am whatever He wants me to be. I cannot say that I am not a writer. As a Christian, I am whoever and whatever God wants me to be. I am His servant. God calls us to do things that we cannot even fathom. I am absolutely nothing and totally worthless without Him living through me. But with Him living through me, He can do anything, even move a mountain. Matthew 17:19-21 says, "Then the disciples came to Jesus in private and asked, 'Why couldn't we drive it out?' He replied, 'Because you have so little faith. I tell you the truth, if you have faith as small as a mustard seed, you can say to this mountain, 'Move from here to there' and it will move. Nothing will be impossible for you.'" Did you see that? Nothing, absolutely nothing is impossible with God.

I will justify my doubts of being a writer by saying that a few years ago, my idea of reading was looking at a magazine. I was never a very quick reader and was even in those "slower" reading groups in elementary school. Therefore, I chose not to read much other than required books in school. (Yes, I read my Bible but that was the extent of my book reading for many years.) Several years ago, God gave me a hunger for more knowledge of Him so I started reading. One would think it ironic that He called me to write a book but God has a good and perfect plan for us. Jeremiah 29:11 tells us, "'For I know the plans I have for you,'" declares the LORD, 'plans to prosper you and not to harm you, plans to give you hope and a future.'" Absolutely nothing is "ironic" with God. He plans every single detail.

Even as I write this, I am thinking that this is crazy for me to even think that I could write a book. I actually have not even told anyone except for my husband because I know it sounds absolutely absurd. I mean, people go to school for this and professional writers spend all of their time writing and I have a full-time job and a family with no extra time. I do not even have a clue about publishing or how to go about this. How could I think that I could complete a book? Well, I cannot write this book but God can write it through me. He has no limits. He is giving me so many things to include that I find myself continually looking for something to write the idea on so I will not forget. Now, I realize that if I continually totally submit this work to God, He will not allow me to forget and He will compile it as He wants. I also realize that God is leading me to write this and I must leave the publishing and everything else in His hands. He is in absolute control and I need not worry, stress or fear because He will guide me.

Why on earth would we think that we could do anything without God? Is God calling you to do something and you are running? Have you submitted everything to God, only to take it back when He did not answer to your liking? His plan is so much better than our plan. We cannot even fathom His perfect plans for us.

Chapter 8:

Why do we despair?

❧

Christians often despair because we are not listening to God. I'll give an example of how we sometimes miss God's voice. I was preparing for a business trip last year. I prayed that morning for God to use me to witness to someone on the plane that day. (How arrogant for me to tell God how He should use me!) I was reading a Christian book on the plane and I waited for the opportunity to share and it never came. So, I wondered why God didn't use me. (Again, I know, arrogant!)

I reached my destination and checked in the hotel. I walked around and found some shops near the hotel. As I was returning to the hotel and talking on my cell phone, a homeless man approached me asking for money. I refused as I usually do. (I worked on a psychiatric unit for many years and I met way too many patients who told me how easy it was to get money for drugs and alcohol. I would have no part of giving someone cash because they would probably use it for drugs and alcohol. Of course, that was an extremely judgmental attitude but I thought I justified it well. Oh, how I was deceiving myself!) I was also walking alone in a strange city and thought it would be unsafe to stop and look for money. (Again, I was justifying my every action!)

I returned to my hotel room and God convicted me. I fell to my knees. That homeless man was my opportunity that I had prayed for to witness to someone that day. It didn't appear as I had thought it should so I did not look anywhere else. I felt horrible because I had been so hardened that I did not even see God's answer to the prayer request I had that very morning. I had planned to not leave the room again that night but I prayed for God to forgive me and I asked for another chance.

My phone rang and it was a co-worker who had felt ill and asked me to walk with her to the closest store. She did not want to walk alone and I had already been out and knew where the shops were located. So, I walked with her. On the return to the hotel, a different homeless man approached and requested money. Again, I said "no" and we kept walking. God immediately convicted me. I had asked for a second chance and I blew it again! How could I be so blind? I hurriedly got my money and ran down the street. Yes, I chased the homeless man down and gave him money and with tears in my eyes, I said "God bless you." (I'm certain that he thought that I must be a crazy lady chasing him down the street to give him money.)

Matthew 25:35-40 says, "'For I was hungry and you gave me something to eat, I was thirsty and you gave me something to drink, I was a stranger and you invited me in, I needed clothes and you clothed me, I was sick and you looked after me, I was in prison and you came to visit me.' Then the righteous will answer him, 'Lord, when did we see you hungry and feed you, or thirsty and give you something to drink? When did we see you a stranger and invite you in, or needing clothes and clothe you? When did we see you sick or in prison and go to visit you?' The King will reply,

'I tell you the truth, whatever you did for one of the least of these brothers of mine, you did for me.'"

I realize that was a long story but there are several points to that story. One point is that although we think that we are in control, we are not. God is in control. He knows the past, present and future and He is in total control. A second point is that we can never tell God how to use us. He does not need us. We need Him but He chooses to use us and bless us through it. The third point is that although we think we are walking close to God and we are listening to Him, we do not always hear what He is saying.

Christians should never despair because we are God's children and we will spend eternity in heaven. However, non-Christians should despair because they will spend eternity in hell. Ephesians 5:5-7 says, "For of this you can be sure: No immoral, impure or greedy person—such a man is an idolater—has any inheritance in the kingdom of Christ and of God. Let no one deceive you with empty words, for because of such things God's wrath comes on those who are disobedient. Therefore do not be partners with them." Where is your inheritance?

1 Corinthians 6:9-11 tells us, "Do you not know that the wicked will not inherit the kingdom of God? Do not be deceived: Neither the sexually immoral nor idolaters nor adulterers nor male prostitutes nor homosexual offenders nor thieves nor the greedy nor drunkards nor slanderers nor swindlers will inherit the kingdom of God. And that is what some of you were. But you were washed, you were sanctified, you were justified in the name of the Lord Jesus Christ and by the Spirit of our God." Have you been washed and sanctified?

Matthew 7:21-27 says, "Not everyone who says to me, 'Lord, Lord,' will enter the kingdom of heaven, but only he who does the will of my Father who is in heaven. Many will say to me on that day, 'Lord, Lord, did we not prophesy in your name, and in your name drive out demons and perform many miracles?' Then I will tell them plainly, 'I never knew you. Away from me, you evildoers! Therefore everyone who hears these words of mine and puts them into practice is like a wise man who built his house on the rock. The rain came down, the streams rose, and the winds blew and beat against that house; yet it did not fall, because it had its foundation on the rock. But everyone who hears these words of mine and does not put them into practice is like a foolish man who built his house on sand. The rain came down, the streams rose, and the winds blew and beat against that house, and it fell with a great crash.'" Is your house built on the rock or is your house built on the sand? Don't you want assurance that you are going to heaven? You can have that assurance today.

The battle is already over and Jesus won! Praise the Lord! Truly, as Christians, we do not have to despair over anything in this world, nothing. We have Jesus living in us and He has already defeated Satan. There is nothing to worry about. No one can defeat us. Oh, yes, Satan will try but whatever he means to harm us, God will turn it around and make it glorious. No matter what has happened to you or whatever you have done in this cruel, dark world, God loves each and every one of us and He wants us to give everything to Him. Everything includes the good, the bad, and the ugly. He will pick up all of our pieces and make something beautiful of our lives.

Revelation 21:4 says, "He will wipe every tear from their eyes. There will be no more death or mourning or crying or pain, for the old order of things has passed away." How awesome is that? Our loving, heavenly Father will wipe away every single tear from our eyes. There will be no despair. Although we live in a dying world that is full of despair, Christians have hope in God and we do not need to despair. We must learn to keep our focus on God and not look around at our circumstances. Satan will try to keep our focus on our surroundings but Satan has already been defeated.

We often despair because we want to have a "pity party... poor, pitiful me...look what happened to me...it's all about me, me, me." Buck up! Get over yourself! Do you find yourself constantly saying "it's just not fair"? Well, life is not fair. (Just ask my children how many times a day that I share that with them!) This life is temporary. Christians have a heavenly home awaiting us. We all need to keep our eyes on Jesus and allow Him to fill us with His love, peace and joy. John 14:27 says, "Peace I leave with you; my peace I give you. I do not give to you as the world gives. Do not let your hearts be troubled and do not be afraid."

We cannot put our faith and hope in humans because they will always let us down. Psalm 62:5 says, "Find rest, O my soul, in God alone; my hope comes from him." God will never let us down. Hebrews 13:5-6 tells us, "Keep your lives free from the love of money and be content with what you have, because God has said, 'Never will I leave you; never will I forsake you.' So we say with confidence, 'The Lord is my helper; I will not be afraid. What can man do to me?'"

This dying world desperately needs His light. Does your co-worker or friend even know that you are a Christian? What do people think of when they think of you? Do they think of you as a complainer or a positive person, happy or sad, gossip or not, a problem or solution? Do you go to church on Sunday morning and leave God there until next Sunday?

Christians, let's take a stand! Let God do a work in each and every one of us. Let His light shine through you for the whole world to see. 1 John 1:5-9 says, "This is the message we have heard from him and declare to you: God is light; in him there is no darkness at all. If we claim to have fellowship with him yet walk in the darkness, we lie and do not live by the truth. But if we walk in the light, as he is in the light, we have fellowship with one another, and the blood of Jesus, his Son, purifies us from all sin. If we claim to be without sin, we deceive ourselves and the truth is not in us. If we confess our sins, he is faithful and just and will forgive us our sins and purify us from all unrighteousness."

Christians have overcome the world. 1 John 4:4-5 tells us, "You, dear children, are from God and have overcome them, because the one who is in you is greater than the one who is in the world. They are from the world and therefore speak from the viewpoint of the world, and the world listens to them."

We despair because we look around at this dying world. There is still hope for this dying world. This country asks where God is when bad things happen. God never moves. We move. We, as a country, have rejected God and turned our backs on Him. If Christians would bind together and seek God's will, God will hear us and He will turn His wrath away from us. 2 Chronicles 7:14 tells us, "If my people, who are called by my name, will humble themselves and pray and seek my face and turn from their wicked ways, then will I hear from heaven and will forgive their sin and will heal their land." Let's be obedient to His word and He will heal our land. Christians do not need to lose hope nor do we need to give up on others. We are to love everyone as Jesus loves us. We need to pray continually for each other and for our country. It is never too late with God.

Our heavenly blessings awaiting us are so much better than anything that we may perceive as an earthly treasure. We must wait patiently on Him. Psalm 27:14 says, "Wait for the Lord; be strong and take heart and wait for the Lord." Psalm 33:20 tells us, "We wait in hope for the Lord; He is our help and our shield."

Isaiah 40:31 tells us, "but those who hope in the Lord will renew their strength. They will soar on wings like eagles; they will run and not grow weary, they will walk and not be faint." We will soar like eagles and not grow weary and not be faint. Yes, in this fast-paced busy life, we will not grow weary. Joshua 1:9 says, "Have I not commanded you? Be strong and courageous. Do not be terrified; do not be discouraged, for the Lord your God will be with you wherever you go." We are not to be discouraged about anything. God is always with us and God is bigger than any problem that we may face.

1 John 5:14-15 tells us, "This is the confidence we have in approaching God: that if we ask anything according to his will, he hears us. And if we know that he hears us—whatever we ask—we know that we have what we asked of him." Now, we have to be sure that we are asking according to His will and not our own will. His will is always better than our will. We cannot even imagine what He has awaiting us and we can have it if we only ask.

Philippians 4:19 says, "And my God will meet all your needs according to his glorious riches in Christ Jesus." Yes, He will meet all of our needs. He will never leave us nor forsake us. He sent His only son into this dying world to save us from our sins. He loves us that much. We can never do anything to deserve His love or to deserve eternity in heaven. Jesus already paid the price on the cross for us. 1 Timothy 1:14 says, "The grace of our Lord was poured out on me abundantly, along with the faith and love that are in Christ Jesus." He has abundantly poured out his grace and love upon us. We just have to accept it and be obedient to Him.

Chapter 9:

Forgiveness always conquers bitterness and anger.

I know people who have been through terrible heartache and no, they did not do anything to deserve the pain. Some have lost family members and friends, some have gone through a bitter divorce and custody battle, some have physical/mental illnesses, some have been abused, and some have family discord. Let us not forget about substance abuse which is so rampant today and the many other addictions that are prevalent including sexual addictions. The list is endless. Everywhere there are people hurting. If they would make the choice to let God heal them, they would have joy and peace; however, so many of these people choose to live with bitterness and anger. Psalm 147:3 tells us, "He healeth the broken in heart and bindeth up their wounds." (KJV)

I know what some are going to say. I can hear it now. "Well, you don't know what I've been through." You are right. I do not know and I will not pretend to know. But I can assure you that God knows and He cares. Look at what Jesus went through. He gave up His Heavenly Kingdom to come and live in this cruel, harsh world. He knew what was going to happen to Him and He did it anyway. He lived a perfect, sinless life and then died a sinner's death on the cross for you and me. He suffered the pain of not having contact with God while on the cross because He chose to take on our sin. He became sin so that we could have everlasting life.

He loves us that much. We cannot imagine how much He suffered while living on earth. He did it for us. He went through all of those trials in human form so that He could bear our burdens. He understands what you are going through and He wants to provide you comfort and healing. He will guide us every step of the way if we will just seek Him. Psalms 32:8 says, "I will instruct you and teach you in the way you should go; I will counsel you and watch over you."

I could choose to be angry and bitter at Dennis for the rest of my life. What would that do to me or him or our children? It would build up in me and cause me to be a hardened, bitter, angry person that could not be used for God's Kingdom. And, who would want to be around me? I would not be able to stand to be around myself. Really, who likes to be around people who are constantly bitter and angry at the world? Would my anger and bitterness help Dennis? No. Would it help our children? No. It helps no one. It only hinders our sweet fellowship with God and any relationships that we have. Satan wants us to remain bitter so that we cannot be used by God.

Forgiveness is a command not an option. Matthew 18:21-25 tells us, "Then Peter came to Jesus and asked, 'Lord, how many times shall I forgive my brother when he sins against me? Up to seven times?' Jesus answered, 'I tell you, not seven times, but seventy-seven times.' Therefore, the kingdom of heaven is like a king who wanted to settle accounts with his servants. As he began the settlement, a man who owed him ten thousand talents was brought to him. Since he was not able to pay, the master ordered that he and his wife and his children and all that he had be sold to repay the debt. The servant fell on his knees before him. 'Be patient with me,' he begged, 'and I will pay back everything.' The servant's master took pity on him, canceled the debt and let him go. But when that servant went out, he found one of his fellow servants who owed him a hundred denarii. He grabbed him and began to choke him. 'Pay back what you owe me!' he demanded. "His fellow servant fell to his knees and begged him, 'Be patient with me, and I will pay you back.' But he refused. Instead, he went off and had the man thrown into prison until he could pay the debt. When the other servants saw what had happened, they were greatly distressed and went and told their master everything that had happened. Then the master called the servant in. 'You wicked servant,' he said, 'I canceled all that debt of yours because you begged me to. Shouldn't you have had mercy on your fellow servant just as I had on you?' In anger his master turned him over to the jailers to be tortured, until he should pay back all he owed. This is how my heavenly Father will treat each of you unless you forgive your brother from your heart."

Sometimes we tell people that we have forgiven them when we actually are just saying that because we know that it is the right thing to do and we have no intention of truly forgiving them. Have you truly forgiven from your heart? Remember that God knows our hearts and we cannot hide anything from Him. He knows if you have forgiven whoever has wronged you.

Many people believe that whoever wronged them does not deserve to be forgiven. We do not deserve to be forgiven of our sins either but God still forgives us. Our society also tends to want to get revenge. Our natural instinct is to try to get revenge. Would I have benefited anyone if I would have thrown all of Dennis' belongings out in the yard and changed the locks on the door? No! This would have caused bitterness and hatred. Leviticus 19:18 says, "'Do not seek revenge or bear a grudge against one of your people, but love your neighbor as yourself. I am the Lord.'"

Although our prayers should be for the person who hurt us to repent and turn to God, if they do not repent, then God's revenge will come down on them. God's revenge is far worse than our revenge could ever be. Romans 12:17-21 tells us, "Do not repay anyone evil for evil. Be careful to do what is right in the eyes of everybody. If it is possible, as far as it depends on you, live at peace with everyone. Do not take revenge, my friends, but leave room for God's wrath, for it is written: 'It is mine to avenge; I will repay,' says the Lord. On the contrary: 'If your enemy is hungry, feed him; if he is thirsty, give him something to drink. In doing this, you will heap burning coals on his head.' Do not be overcome by evil, but overcome evil with good."

Some may say that they simply cannot forgive the person who hurt them so deeply. I am certain that there is no possible way that I could forgive Dennis for everything that he has done without God's strength. It is just not humanly possible but anything is possible with God. God will give you the strength to forgive. Colossians 3:13 tells us, "Bear with each other and forgive whatever grievances you may have against one another. Forgive as the Lord forgave you." Have you forgiven as the Lord has forgiven you?

Psalm 37:7-8 says, "Be still before the Lord and wait patiently for him; do not fret when men succeed in their ways, when they carry out their wicked schemes. Refrain from anger and turn from wrath; do not fret—it leads only to evil." Exodus 14:14 says, "The Lord will fight for you; you need only to be still." Wow. All we have to do is be still and He will fight for us.

Matthew 5:38-42 says, "You have heard that it was said, 'Eye for eye, and tooth for tooth.' But I tell you, do not resist an evil person. If someone strikes you on the right cheek, turn to him the other also. And if someone wants to sue you and take your tunic, let him have your cloak as well. If someone forces you to go one mile, go with him two miles. Give to the one who asks you, and do not turn away from the one who wants to borrow from you." What if every professing Christian actually lived these verses? Would we see a change in this dying world?

Matthew 7:12 says, "So in everything, do to others what you would have them do to you, for this sums up the Law and the Prophets." Do you treat others the way that you want to be treated? Do you forgive others the way that you want God to forgive you? Job 5:2-3 says, "Resentment kills a fool, and envy slays the simple. I myself have seen a fool taking root, but suddenly his house was cursed." Are you making the choice right now to hold resentment against anyone?

Romans 12:9-13 says, "Love must be sincere. Hate what is evil; cling to what is good. Be devoted to one another in brotherly love. Honor one another above yourselves. Never be lacking in zeal, but keep your spiritual fervor, serving the Lord. Be joyful in hope, patient in affliction, faithful in prayer. Share with God's people who are in need. Practice hospitality." Does this scripture describe you? Do those closest to you feel that this scripture describes you?

Ephesians 4:31-32 tells us, "Get rid of all bitterness, rage and anger, brawling and slander, along with every form of malice. Be kind and compassionate to one another, forgiving each other, just as in Christ God forgave you." Now, remember, Christians, this is all straight from the Bible. The Bible was not written for us to pick and choose which scripture that we want to believe. 2 Timothy 3:16-17 says, "All Scripture is God-breathed and is useful for teaching, rebuking, correcting and training in righteousness, so that the man of God may be thoroughly equipped for every good work." God provided us with the Bible to guide us to live as He has called us to live. Will you choose to accept the Bible as your life instruction manual and read it and memorize it and keep it in your heart?

Chapter 10:

Make the choice this moment to "let go and let God".

೭൨ぉ

As we come to a close in this book, I want to re-empha-size that Christians do have hope in this lonely, dying world. Hope is in God and God alone. The outcome is totally in His hands and He will bless us beyond measure. Habakkuk 3:18 says, "Yet I will rejoice in the Lord, I will be joyful in God my Savior." We must keep our focus on Him and Him alone. We must pray continually, read His Word, be still, and wait for His guidance. Psalm 32:8 tells us, "I will instruct you and teach you in the way you should go; I will counsel you and watch over you." He will guide us if we will only allow Him. 1 Thessalonians 5:16-18 says, "Be joyful always; pray continually; give thanks in all circumstances, for this is God's will for you in Christ Jesus."

Romans 10:9-13 says, "That if you confess with your mouth, 'Jesus is Lord,' and believe in your heart that God raised him from the dead, you will be saved. For it is with your heart that you believe and are justified, and it is with your mouth that you confess and are saved. As the Scripture says, 'Anyone who trusts in him will never be put to shame.' For there is no difference between Jew and Gentile—the same Lord is Lord of all and richly blesses all who call on him, for, 'Everyone who calls on the name of the Lord will be saved.'" Are you certain of your salvation?

Why do Christians mope around with the attitude of "woe is me"? The victory is already won! Christians should be joyous all the time because no matter what is going on around us, we have eternal life in heaven. We have no reason to despair. We are His children. John 1:12 says, "Yet to all who received him, to those who believed in his name, he gave the right to become children of God."

Christians, will you allow God to transform you? 2 Corinthians 3:18 says, "And we, who with unveiled faces all reflect the Lord's glory, are being transformed into his likeness with ever-increasing glory, which comes from the Lord, who is the Spirit." 1 John 2:3-6 says, "We know that we have come to know him if we obey his commands. The man who says, 'I know him,' but does not do what he commands is a liar, and the truth is not in him. But if anyone obeys His word, God's love is truly made complete in him. This is how we know we are in him: Whoever claims to live in him must walk as Jesus did."

Don't settle for anything this world has to offer. Only accept God's perfect will for your life. Is your momentary pleasure on this earth really worth eternity in hell? Don't allow Satan to rule over you. He doesn't care about you. He is deceitful. He is using you and only seeks to kill and destroy you. We desperately need to turn from Satan and seek God. Hebrews 4:16 says, "Let us then approach the throne of grace with confidence, so that we may receive mercy and find grace to help us in our time of need."

Romans 12:2 says, "Do not conform any longer to the pattern of this world, but be transformed by the renewing of your mind. Then you will be able to test and approve what God's will is—his good, pleasing and perfect will." James 1:22-25 says, "Do not merely listen to the word, and so deceive yourselves. Do what it says. Anyone who listens to the word but does not do what it says is like a man who looks at his face in a mirror and, after looking at himself, goes away and immediately forgets what he looks like. But the man who looks intently into the perfect law that gives freedom, and continues to do this, not forgetting what he has heard, but doing it—he will be blessed in what he does."

Christians have blended in with the world so much that our neighbors and friends do not even know that we are Christians. We are so busy in this world pursuing earthly pleasures that we forget the one true reason that we are on this earth, to serve our Lord and Savior. James 4:4 says, "You adulterous people, don't you know that friendship with the world is hatred toward God? Anyone who chooses to be a friend of the world becomes an enemy of God." Have you made the choice to be a friend of the world? Then you are an enemy of God. But, it is not too late to choose God. Ephesians 2:10 says, "For we are God's workmanship, created in Christ Jesus to do good works, which God prepared in advance for us to do."

For unbelievers, you can make the choice right now to become a Christian. You can have the assurance this very minute that you will spend eternity in heaven no matter what your past holds. Acts 4:12 says, "Salvation is found in no one else, for there is no other name under heaven given to men by which we must be saved." 1 John 1:9 tells us, "If we confess our sins, he is faithful and just and will forgive us our sins and purify us from all unrighteousness."

You have a choice to make today. Either you can give it all to God and let Him transform you or you can put this book down and get caught up in the busyness of life around you. You cannot serve 2 masters and you cannot be luke-warm. Who will you choose to serve?

Hebrews 11:6 says, "And without faith it is impossible to please God, because anyone who comes to him must believe that he exists and that he rewards those who earnestly seek him." Do you have faith? 1 Peter 5:10-11 says, "And the God of all grace, who called you to his eternal glory in Christ, after you have suffered a little while, will Himself restore you and make you strong, firm and steadfast. To him be the power forever and ever. Amen." He will restore us! There is no maybe or can in there. He will Himself restore us. Praise the Lord!

Philippians 1:6 tells us, "being confident of this, that he who began a good work in you will carry it on to completion until the day of Christ Jesus." No matter the mess that we have made of our lives, He will complete the good work in us. We have God, the Creator of the Universe, with us. What more could we possibly want or need?

1 Corinthians 2:9 says, "However, as it is written: 'No eye has seen, no ear has heard, no mind has conceived what God has prepared for those who love him.'" We cannot even conceive what He has prepared for us! He is amazing. Psalm 128:1 tells us, "Blessed are all who fear the Lord, who walk in his ways." Do you fear God or do you just go on about your business and expect Him to forgive you because He is a loving God? Oh what a chance you are taking if you do not fear and revere Him!

We only have to follow Him and He will never leave us. We can ask Him anything and we have complete certainty that He will always answer us and He will always provide for us. We need never fear anything in this world. Jeremiah 33:3 tells us, "Call to me and I will answer you and tell you great and unsearchable things you do not know."

We all have foolish days. We all sin and make mistakes. It is what we do with those sins and mistakes that make the difference. Do we give them to God and turn from them or do we choose to continue in them and ignore God? 1 Corinthians 1:25 says, "For the foolishness of God is wiser than man's wisdom, and the weakness of God is stronger than man's strength." Wow. We are absolutely nothing…we are worthless in comparison to God. But with God we can be anything and do anything that He leads us to be and do. His name alone is power.

Could you be the one with the hardened heart and blinded by Satan? If you have read this book and feel nothing applies to you, pray and ask for God to reveal any sin in your life that has broken sweet fellowship with Him. We all sin every day. If you have never received Christ as your savior, please pray right now and ask Jesus to forgive you of your sins and to live in your heart. Seek a local church immediately to become a member of a church family so you can grow as a believer. God will give you a mountaintop experience in the midst of the valley if you will allow Him. He is waiting on you with His arms open wide. Will you choose Him?

LaVergne, TN USA
11 July 2010
189066LV00003B/39/P